To Helen & Milt BARNETT

from

Di & Jack

Christmas 1978.

The Cape Cod Canal

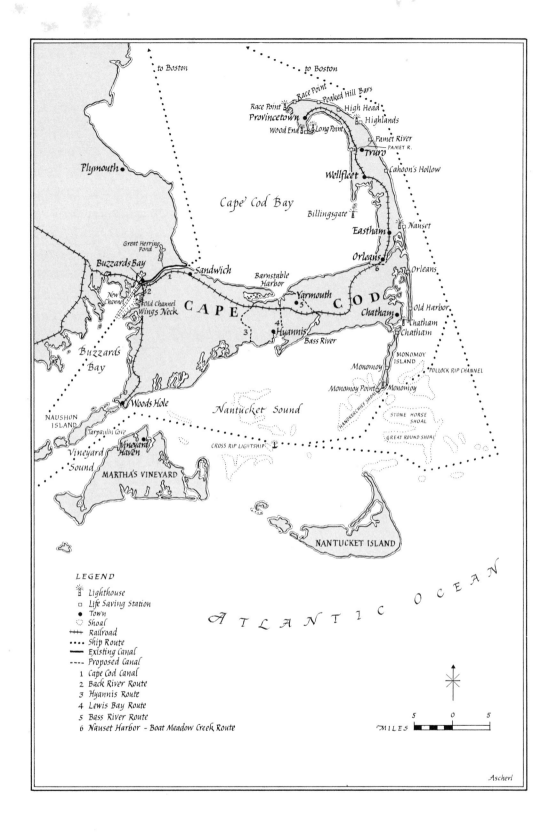

to Boston

to Boston

Race Point

Race Point
Peaked Hill Bars
High Head
Provincetown
Highlands
Wood End
Long Point
Pamet River
PAMET R.
Truro

Plymouth

Cape Cod Bay

Wellfleet
Cahoon's Hollow

Billingsgate

Eastham
Nauset

Great Herring
Pond

Orleans

Buzzards Bay
Orleans

Sandwich

1

Barnstable
Harbor

CAPE

COD

6

New
Channel

2

Old Channel
Wings Neck

Yarmouth
5

Old Harbor

Chatham
Chatham
Chatham

3

4
Hyannis

Bass River

Buzzards
Bay

MONOMOY
ISLAND

POLLOCK RIP CHANNEL

Monomoy

Woods Hole

Monomoy Point
Monomoy

NAUSHON
ISLAND

Nantucket Sound

HANDKERCHIEF SHOAL

STONE HORSE
SHOAL

Tarpaulin Cove

Vineyard
Haven

CROSS RIP LIGHTSHIP

GREAT ROUND SHOAL

Vineyard

Sound

MARTHA'S VINEYARD

NANTUCKET ISLAND

A T L A N T I C   O C E A N

LEGEND

Lighthouse
Life Saving Station
Town
Shoal
Railroad
Ship Route
Existing Canal
Proposed Canal
1 Cape Cod Canal
2 Back River Route
3 Hyannis Route
4 Lewis Bay Route
5 Bass River Route
6 Nauset Harbor - Boat Meadow Creek Route

5   0   5
MILES

Ascherl

The
CAPE COD
CANAL

by ROBERT H. FARSON

WESLEYAN UNIVERSITY PRESS

MIDDLETOWN · CONNECTICUT

Copyright © 1977 by Wesleyan University

Library of Congress Cataloging in Publication Data

Farson, Robert H   1923–
    The Cape Cod Canal.

    Bibliography: p.
      1. Cape Cod Ship Canal—History.   I. Title.
HE396.C3F37   386'.47'094492   77–74558
ISBN 0–8195–5012–4
ISBN 0–8195–6050–2 pbk.

Manufactured in the United States of America

To Joan, Kris, Greg, Robin, Matt, and Jeff

Contents

List of Illustrations

Acknowledgments

The single most helpful resource in my research has been William James Reid's Ph.D. dissertation on the Cape Cod Canal. Dr. Reid's bibliography is the most complete list of sources on the subject. I used it extensively and acknowledge my considerable debt to his work.

I am indebted also to many people for their assistance and encouragement throughout the preparation of this book, the idea of which grew out of three visits I had with Cape Codders.

The first visit was to the Aptuxcet Trading Post on the canal in Bourne, where Mrs. George Hiltwein explained the collections there.

A search for Fred Small's glass negatives took me to the Bourne Historical Society's collection nearby at Elizabeth Bourne's home. Richard Bourne Sanborn had photographic copies made from the negatives for me.

Several days later I talked to Benjamin S. Harrison of the Village of Buzzards Bay. Ben provided me with hundreds of photographs and a great deal of information over a period of three years.

The outstanding collection of construction photos, contracts, newspapers, and copies of speeches in the Sandwich Public Library was once the property of Mrs. Harold S. Andrew, whose husband was an engineer with the Cape Cod Construction Company. Louise Walker, the librarian, made the collection available for my use.

Russell A. Lovell, Jr. showed me the canal material in the Sandwich Historical Society and gave me a copy of his article on tides of the Atlantic Coast and how they affect the canal.

Nancy O. Merrill, director-curator of the Sandwich Historical Society, made available to me the maps and photographs in that large collection.

Many of the excellent marine photographs in this book were found by Alice and Jim Wilson in the huge files of the Steamship Historical Society of America in Baltimore.

William D. Donovan, a marine traffic controller who has guided hundreds of thousands of ships through the Cape Cod Canal, loaned me photographs of many of them and explained their significance to this story.

Robert F. Smalley, also a marine traffic controller, patiently showed me how the canal operates in an age of electronics. He made it look easy, although it is far from that.

Data and photographs from United States government files were provided by Walter Mackie, public information officer of the New England Division, Army Corps of Engineers, Waltham, Massachusetts.

From his superb maritime collection, R. Loren Graham sent me many photographs that are in this work, besides a vast amount of information.

The copying of many hundreds of photographs and maps was done by Edward C. Robinson, who also took some pictures for this book.

Robert Hollister supplied information from many old newspapers.

Thanks are also due to those unnamed librarians and their assistants at Harvard University, Columbia University, the Pennsylvania State University, and the Boston Public Library.

Professor Donald L. Smith, of the School of Journalism of the Pennsylvania State University, edited the manuscript with great care.

The suggestions of Steve Auerweck helped to clarify things.

My wife Joan was not only willing to have the Cape Cod Canal moved into our home, but she typed many captions for the photographs.

To all of you—many thanks.

The Cape Cod Canal

Introduction

AFTER a week of rain the skies had cleared. During the past month many people had been buying colored cotton bunting and flags to decorate their homes and businesses. That morning the decorations had been put up on houses, shops, and factories from Buzzards Bay to Sandwich. A railroad car plant at Sagamore looked especially festive.

Later in the day people started to arrive; they came by themselves, with friends, or with family. They came by car or train; they came on foot, or they rode in buggies or on horseback. They came to see what for them was a great event: the Cape Cod Canal was about to open with a parade of ships. It was Wednesday, July 29, 1914.

By early afternoon their numbers had grown to thousands. Through a fleet of hundreds of smaller craft in Buzzards Bay, they saw a line of larger vessels, led by a white excursion steamer with her paddle wheels churning. The S.S. *Rose Standish* of Boston, her whistle sending skyward plumes of steam, rounded Gray Gables Point, once the site of the summer home of Pres. Grover Cleveland. Now those along the shore could see her crowded decks and the waving arms. They waved back and cheered. At 1:31 P.M., one minute behind schedule, the *Rose Standish's* bow sliced through a piece of bunting that was hung across the canal. Following this symbolic cutting of the ribbon came the other ships: destroyers, yachts, and a tugboat for the press.

The ships passed, and many people along the banks cranked up their automobile engines and chased the fleet eastward, driving down the narrow roads parallel to the new waterway. For the older Cape Codders it must have been hard to believe, since for a far longer time than they could recall there had been talk of and planning for a canal across the isthmus to link the waters of Buzzards Bay with those of Cape Cod Bay. After nearly three centuries, a Cape Cod canal—the first proposed public work in the American colonies—was open.

The cape itself had an awesome beginning. At the end of the last Ice Age—about ten thousand years ago—it was formed from the rocks and soil of northern New England slowly carried to the coast and dropped there by a melting glacier. Geologists call it a terminal moraine. When the ice retreated, the ocean and the wind went to work, shaping what the glacier left and polishing it into a peninsula sixty-five miles long and from one to twenty miles wide. Sixteen miles south of Plymouth, the cape is part of the coastal lowlands and gentle hills that are sprinkled with dozens of lakes and ponds formed by huge ice chunks from the retreating glacier. Wide sandy beaches and dunes dominate the landscape. Along its shores numerous tidal creeks wind their way through salt marshes.

This famous land formation was described by naturalist Henry David Thoreau: "Cape Cod is the bared and bended arm of Massachusetts; the shoulder is at Buzzards Bay; the elbow, or crazy-bone is at Cape Mallebarre; the wrist at Truro; and the sandy fist at Provincetown. . . ."

Today Cape Cod is an island, bounded by the Atlantic Ocean to the east; Nantucket Sound to the south; Cape Cod Bay to the north and inside the forearm; the protected inlet of Buzzards Bay to the west; and the Cape Cod Canal, running in a northeast-southwest direction through a broad valley where the shoulder joins the mainland of southeastern Massachusetts.

This attractive land, whose air mixes the smells of salt water and pitch pine, draws millions of tourists, crowding its antique shops, museums, and art galleries. They swim, picnic, and fish. And they talk about the cape's quaintness: the narrow lanes, church spires, picket fences, climbing roses, single-story houses with wooden clapboards and weathered shingles. Increasingly they find commercial strips—gas stations, gift shops with imported junk, ice cream and candy stands, franchised fast-food restaurants, motels with small swimming pools, blacktopped parking lots, and, everywhere, signs.

This is all a far cry from what the first Europeans saw when they ventured along the East Coast. About A.D. 1000 the cape may have been visited by Norsemen, as it is believed to be among the many places on the eastern seaboard investigated by those intrepid deep-water voyagers. Other early explorers probably sailed to the cape and some of them may have come ashore, but it was not until the spring of 1602 when the British navigator Bartholomew Gosnold sailed down the coast from Maine to Buzzards Bay that there was any written mention of the cape. Gosnold spent a little more than one month there, meeting with the Indians and cutting down trees to build a house and a fort. His fishing success inspired him to give Cape Cod its name. Three years later the Frenchman Samuel Champlain made his first visit to the cape, returning the following year. In late fall of 1620 the Pilgrims arrived, stopping for about one month at the northern tip of the cape, its "sandy fist," before crossing the bay to build their colony at Plymouth.

Miles Standish, Plymouth Colony's military officer, made many trips down the coast. He discovered a valley the Indians used to portage their small boats across the isthmus at the cape's shoulder, thus avoiding the dangerous shoals and rough waters outside. As the valley at its highest point was only twenty-nine feet above sea level, Standish and his men sailed up a small river from Cape Cod Bay to it and dragged their craft over the sand until they reached a creek that drained westward into Buzzards Bay. He suggested a canal be dug through the valley, connecting the two bays, and his idea, the first American public work project, was debated at Plymouth. Its cost, of course, was beyond the means of the small colony, but the idea of a through waterway was born; its prospects would excite many others as it had excited these early European settlers.

To avoid the dangers of sailing around the cape other canal routes were proposed, but the first one, through the valley of the isthmus, was the principal one considered. And it was there that the canal was finally built. For nearly three centuries engineers tramped down the valley and back and elsewhere on the cape. Numerous groups who wanted to build a canal, or said they did, were granted charters by the Massachusetts General Court (the legislature). At one time the fighting over who would get the charters became so intense that a Harvard University historian, Henry C. Kittredge, wrote: "If ever a strip of land was a parade-ground for surveyors first and a battle-ground for legislative vituperation afterwards, it was the route of the Cape Cod Canal." The charter-seekers were a variety of dreamers, talkers, and frauds. The last person to get a charter finally found a man who would actually build a canal, and that is a major part of this story.

But why such an interest in buiding a canal across the cape? During the American Revolution the British navy was in command of the outside waters of the cape, thus limiting the movements of General Washington's Continental navy. American military supplies had to be portaged through the valley then and again during the War of 1812 by blockade runners. Clearly the exposed course around the cape constituted a chink in the nation's armor. Besides the military advantages of a short, safe route, canal proponents stressed its commercial and humanitarian blessings.

With the rise of technological society during the nineteenth century and the resulting industrial growth, transportation became critical. Faster and more reliable means of moving products and people were imperative. Canal boats towed by horses gave way to railroad cars pulled by locomotives, while sailing vessels were giving way, though reluctantly, to steamboats. The coastal merchant fleet mushroomed during the nineteenth century, when most goods and materials for New England's expanding industry moved by water. Because of the area's coastal topography with its numerous bays and rivers, the location of cities and towns on tidewater favored ocean transport even after the railroads came. Shipbuilding was a mainstay. In some centers it was the principal industry, and every port had at least one shipyard.

The surging industrial growth of New England created great demands for lumber, much of it from southern forests. It came north by ship. Water power proved unreliable as an energy source, and industry needed an inexpensive replacement. At first it was Pennsylvania anthracite and—later—bituminous coal. The demand for coal was incessant, but mine operators uncovered more in Maryland, Virginia, and West Virginia. It, too, reached New England's hungry furnaces by ship. Along with lumber and coal, cotton and agricultural products were carried north by water and high-grade manufactures went south. By the 1890s more than thirty thousand ships per year rounded Cape Cod; there were steamers, schooners and square-riggers, United States Navy vessels, fishing boats, yachts, and strings of coastal barges so long that the last ships could not even be seen from the tugboats towing them. Some of the deeper draught vessels went outside Nantucket Island. Most of them sailed through Nantucket Sound, a mariner's nightmare of shoals, twisting channels, surging tides and currents, ice, fog, and a long lee shore without ports of refuge. Near the center of Nantucket Sound a lightship marked Cross Rip Shoal. A little to its east the route split between a northeasterly course for Pollock Rip Channel and a due easterly course, passing south of Great Round Shoal. Although it was more dangerous because of congestion, shoals, and turns, most ships used Pollock Rip Channel; it was shorter and less exposed than the more easterly route. Circuitous and narrow in places, the channel was especially dangerous to navigate during heavy storms from the northeast or the southwest. Government charts helped but they were never up to date, since the bottom is irregular and always shifting. Lightships were on station and channels were marked by buoys, but the navigational aids often disappeared after collisions, especially when tugboat captains would swing a line of barges by approaching a turn and then "snapping the whip."

Fog, another natural problem of the area, forms by condensation when cold Maine currents meet warmer water from the south at the cape's elbow off Chatham. At Pollock Rip fog is reported on 130 days per year for a total of 1,100 hours. Through this dense fog steamers moved smartly to stay on schedule, schooners and other wind ships tacked through twisting channels, while coastal tows, some of them over six thousand feet long, ploughed ahead. In clear weather, day or night, it was difficult enough, but in fog or heavy snow it was often treacherous.

In his fine account of a trip on a four-masted coal schooner from Norfolk, Virginia, to Portland, Maine, in 1897, Frederick Sturgis Lawrence recalled sailing through Pollock Rip Channel into "the worst fog I have ever seen." His ship, the *Sarah C. Ropes*, was deeply laden with bituminous. On her way through the channel she struck the sandy bottom three times, causing some anxiety but no damage. "Night was falling and the route from there north was fairly well populated with steamers sailing in both directions," he wrote. "We could hear their whistles moaning to right, to left and in front of us. The fog was so thick that the galley amidships could not be seen from the after cabin house, nor the forecastle head from the galley. A pitifully small squawk issues from a hand operated fog horn on the forecastle head where the lookout was posted." Often, in such conditions, sailing ships would anchor using only dim kerosene lamps and those hand-operated fog horns as warnings. Sometimes the ships would be off to the side or out of the channel. But wherever they anchored there was still a danger of collision, since the steamers kept moving, and the large number of vessels clogged the narrow passages through the shoals. The tensions of navigating Nantucket and Vineyard sounds were so intense that it was common practice for the steamship companies to have their captains work for two weeks and then take one week off. During thick, persistent fog many sailing vessels were held for days at a time in anchorages at Martha's Vineyard and Provincetown. When the fog lifted ships' masters had to be especially alert to the dangers of collision, as every vessel would set out from port at once. An early turn at the coal docks was at stake.

During heavy storms sailing vessels and tows would anchor at Vineyard Haven, waiting for clear skies and a chance to put to sea. But there were always some mariners willing to take a risk, and without accurate weather forecasting and radio to warn captains, many ships were caught in open water and driven onto shoals and beaches. Winter storms were most severe and the bitter cold exhausted sailors already tired from constant duty under harrowing conditions. Ice floes in Nantucket Sound were an added threat.

The United States Life Saving Service, which maintained thirteen stations between Monomoy Point and Wood End, near Provincetown, reported that 687 ships were wrecked between 1875 and 1903. At least one hundred five lives were lost, and vessels and cargoes worth over $2 million were destroyed. In his book *Life Savers of Cape Cod*, John W. Dalton, a *Boston Globe* reporter, wrote:

> Myriads of shoals lie along the coast, and unnumbered vessels have met their doom along its shores, which rightly bear the name "Ocean Graveyard." The shores of Cape Cod from Monomoy to Wood End are literally strewn with the bones of once staunch crafts, while unmarked graves in the burial-places in the villages along the coast mutely relate the sad tale of the sacrifice of human life.

Mariners dreaded the waters around the cape. In its issue of October 25, 1913, the *Marine Journal* called this stretch "the most dangerous coast in winter to be found on the map of the United States."

Thoreau visited the cape four times between 1849 and 1857, and on one of those visits he and his friend, the clergyman and poet William Ellery Channing, walked to the edge of a bluff above the Great Beach near the three Nauset lighthouses. He described the treacherous water below:

> The sea was exceedingly dark and stormy, the sky completely overcast, the clouds still dropping rain, and the wind seemed to blow not so much as the exciting cause, as from sympathy with the already agitated ocean. The waves broke on the bars at some distance from the shore, and curving green or yellow as if over so many unseen dams, ten or twelve feet high, like a thousand waterfalls, rolled in foam to the sand. There was nothing but that savage ocean between us and Europe.

On another occasion, Thoreau was appalled at what he saw following a ship-wreck. He wrote: "The annals of this voracious beach! Who could write them, unless it were a shipwrecked sailor. Think of the amount of suffering that a single strand has witnessed."

A shorter, safer route was the answer to the dangers of sailing around the cape and over the shoals. Fifty years of American inland canal building came and passed by 1840. Ferdinand de Lesseps completed his 100-mile ditch at Suez in 1869, and then tried, and failed, in Panama. The British opened up Manchester to the sea with a canal in 1894. The Germans built their ship canal at Kiel one year later. Still Cape Cod did not have its through waterway, though a flurry of charter applications was received by the General Court in Boston.

Finally in 1899 the last charter to build a Cape Cod canal was granted, although it was ten years before construction began. Five years after ground was broken the first ships sailed through the waterway, just a few weeks before the Panama Canal linked the oceans. The long path to that July afternoon in 1914 is a story of power struggles among the very wealthy and of the haphazard vitality of a booming nation. It is a story of many men working toward, and finally realizing, one dream.

1

From the Pilgrims to 1899:
False Starts and Pipe Dreams

SOON after the Pilgrims landed at Plymouth in 1620 they began barter-
ing with the Narragansett Indians, a friendly people clustered in
thatched huts near the shore. The white men had knives, trinkets, and
other manufactured goods; the Indians provided furs and corn to keep the
colonists alive through the early winters. But the Pilgrims soon tilled their
own fields and set their own traps and began seeking further opportunities
to trade. They traveled over land and water, making contacts with Dutch
traders who had sailed north from New Amsterdam. It was in 1623 when
the military leader of the Plymouth colony, Miles Standish, sailed up the
Scusset River from what is now called Cape Cod Bay, passing flats rich with
clams and small creeks where the Indians fished for eel. He reached the head
waters of the river a few miles inland, then dragged his small boat three
miles down the natural valley he found running westward. There he came
upon a small stream—the Manomet (later known as the Monument)—that
ran down the valley to a bay on the western end of the isthmus.

The Pilgrims and the Dutch met on board their craft in the Manomet
River. They began trading, and by 1627 Gov. William Bradford built the
first trading post for Plymouth Colony. Known as Aptuxcet, it was situated
on the south shore of the mouth of the Manomet just east of the bay. The
colonists made a trail some twenty miles long between there and Plymouth.
But carrying goods over those hilly miles was so difficult Bradford decided
to seek a water route. Though the cape was wide at points, its isthmus was
only about eight miles wide, and almost five of those were navigable. Boats
from Plymouth began sailing down the coast sixteen miles to the Scusset,
crossing the sand bar at the mouth of the river at high tide, and moving up
stream as far as they could go. From there the Pilgrims carried their goods
on their backs to other boats on the Manomet, which brought them to
Aptuxcet. Bradford established the route, he wrote, "to avoyd the compasing
of Cape-Codd and those deangerous shoulds; and to make any vioyage to ye
southward in much shorter time, and with farr less danger." In the centuries

that followed the governor's words were often quoted or echoed by those who advocated a canal across the cape.

Because the ridge dividing the two rivers in the isthmus was less than thirty feet above high water the natural route grew more popular as trade increased. Aptuxcet later disappeared and with it the regular commerce it had fostered. But as other traders and seamen continued to sail the two rivers and to carry cargo those few miles overland, the need for a through waterway to avoid the outer route became increasingly evident.

About fifty years after Aptuxcet was founded, an expression of interest in a canal was reported by a young diarist, Samuel Sewall. The elder Sewall had some horses for pasture at Sandwich, and he sent his son to round them up. While there, young Sewall made a short trip. He made the following entry in his diary: "26 OCTO'R, 1676. Mr. Smith rode with me and showed me the place which some had thought to cut, for to make a passage from the south sea to the north . . . the land very low and level . . . Moniment harbor said to be very good."

The first official action in respect to a canal came twenty-one years later, in 1697, when the Massachusetts General Court passed this resolution:

> WHEREAS, it is thought by many to be very necessary for the preservation of men and estates, and very profitable and usefull to the publick, if a passage be cut through the land at Sandwich from Barnstable [now Cape Cod] Bay, so called, into Monament [Buzzards] Bay, for vessels to pass to and from the western part of this country,
>
> ORDERED, that Mr. John Otis of Barnstable, Capt. William Bassett and Mr. Thomas Smith [Sewall's guide], of Sandwich, be and hereby are appointed to view the place, and make report to this court, at their next sessions, what they judge to be the General Conveniences and Inconveniences that may accrue thereby, and what the charge of the same will be, and probability of effecting thereof.

That order began a tradition that would last almost two centuries—committees, surveys, plans, but no action. There is no record that the committee of three ever reported to the court, either orally or in writing, or that the court explored the matter further at that time.

In 1736, Thomas Prince wrote in his *Annals* that the peninsula of Cape Cod was described as "the place through which there has been a canal talked of this forty years which would be a vast advantage to all the country by saving the long and dangerous passage around the Cape, and through the shoals adjoining." More than thirty years later a letter was published in the

Boston Chronicle of March 7, 1768, again pointing out the need for a canal. The author, Publicus, wondered why the idea had lain dormant so long and argued that such a waterway would save ships, lives, and time while lowering freight rates from New England south. Publicus also urged those who lived near Sandwich to write the *Chronicle* about the practicality and expense of such an undertaking. But no one seems to have bothered; at least no letters appeared in subsequent issues of the newspaper.

During the American Revolution, British navy vessels ranged around the cape and along the East Coast, sinking and capturing American ships and thwarting the maritime ventures of the rebellion. Thus to the ever-present dangers of rounding the cape were added the hazards of war. These new perils stirred the Massachusetts General Court to pass another resolution—its second in seventy-nine years—about the possibility of digging a canal across the isthmus. That resolution, introduced on May 1, 1776, stated:

> WHEREAS it is represented to this court, that a Navigable Canal, may without difficulty, be cut through the Isthmus, which separates Buzzards Bay and Barnstable Bay, whereby the hazardous navigation round Cape Cod, both on account of the shoals, and Enemy, may be prevented; and a Safe communication between the Colony and the Southern Colonies be so far secured.

The General Court suggested that a committee look into the project and retain surveyors and engineers. The House agreed. At last it seemed something would be done, if only because of the war.

Thomas Machin, an excellent engineer then on duty with the Continental Army under Gen. Artemus Ward, was found to investigate the feasibility of the canal. Detached from service briefly, Machin went to Cape Cod, surveyed the route, and wrote a report recommending that a canal be built. It survives as the first known Cape Cod Canal survey.

A seven-and-one-half-mile canal with a depth of fourteen feet could be built, Machin wrote. But, he warned, the slightly higher elevation of the land (about two feet) at Cape Cod Bay over that at Buzzards Bay would combine with the different time of tides at either end to produce "a rapid current" through the waterway. To combat this he recommended installing locks, each with two chambers, at both ends of the canal. Machin estimated it would be necessary to remove a little less than one million cubic yards of material from the isthmus, which, along with construction of the locks and two bridges, would cost about thirty-two thousand pounds. While admitting this was a considerable expense, Machin stressed the project's benefits: "great security" against the British and relief from the natural dangers of sailing around the cape. After recommending that his report be sent to the Continental Congress for consideration, Machin obeyed orders from Gen. George Washington and returned to military duty in New York City on June 10, 1776. His report was filed in Boston.

Soon, however, the rebellious colonies would become the United States, and the young nation's attention would move from the rigors of war to peacetime prosperity. Trade increased and American shipbuilding thrived, sparking an era of internal improvement. By 1790, at least thirty canal companies had been incorporated in eight of the original thirteen states. The next fifty years would see the building of 4,400 miles of American canals. Government money spent on canals, much of it appropriated by states, would total $363 million. The public contributed far more than that—perhaps three times as much—through individual purchases of stock in these companies.

As the canal age grew, companies were formed from New England through the Middle West and as far south as Louisiana. Ground was broken in 1817 for De Witt Clinton's "Big Ditch"—the Erie Canal. Seven years later the mammoth project was completed, stretching from the Hudson River to the Great Lakes at Buffalo. Work on that canal inspired such envy among a group of Philadelphians that they pressed for their own waterway, linking Philadelphia with Pittsburgh and the Great Lakes. And, even though the final route meant a portage over the Alleghenies, they succeeded.

Meanwhile, the hardy seafarers back in New England were busy with their own canals. An interest in opening the Connecticut River to navigation had led to that region's first canal, which was dug by hand in one year starting in 1793. The two-mile South Hadley Falls Canal bypassed a stretch of rapids below Northampton, Massachusetts. The same year work began at South Hadley, Gov. John Hancock of Massachusetts granted a petition to the Middlesex Canal Company to dig a canal from Boston Harbor to Chelmsford on the Merrimack River. Stock, which began selling at twenty-five dollars per share, brought in enough money for digging to begin on September 10, 1794. Loammi Baldwin, an ambitious man from Woburn, was hired as superintendent to construct the twenty-seven-mile channel, completing it in 1803. Later, he would survey a route across the isthmus at Cape Cod.

Even Maine, with its splendid network of rivers, saw construction of a canal from Portland to Sebago Lake. Supporters of the Cumberland and Oxford Canal established a lottery in 1828 to raise $50,000 and eventually opened a bank, some of whose deposits were used for construction of the waterway. The twenty-mile-long canal was completed in 1830, and later a lock enabled ships to move another ten miles along the route. But the Cumberland and Oxford Canal was finally abandoned when the Maine Central Railroad moved in and took away its business. There, as elsewhere, the advent of the iron horse spelt the beginning of the end of canal fever.

The glorious age of canals passed, then, with the sailors of Cape Cod still battling Bradford's "deangerous shoulds." It is not as if no one tried to build a canal. Quite the contrary: surveyors alone must have enlivened Sandwich's economy considerably. But somehow incentive and capital never combined at the right time to produce what almost everyone agreed was necessary.

Local interest in the Cape Cod Canal had surged with the trade boom following the Revolution. The number of vessels sailing around the cape had increased, with a corresponding number of sailors and passengers lost to its shoals and storms. As a result, the Massachusetts General Court passed yet another resolution—this one on March 11, 1791—authorizing the governor to appoint one or more persons to look into the possibility of a canal from Buzzards Bay to Barnstable Bay. That survey was prepared by James Winthrop, a well-known Harvard mathematician. Winthrop waited until good weather in May of that year, then finished his survey in twelve days. Although he did not make any recommendations as Machin had done, Winthrop believed the route through the isthmus, using the Back River on the western end, had potential.

Members of the General Court wanted another opinion, and four months after Winthrop finished his survey, they hired a Philadelphian, John Hills, who came to Sandwich and worked several months. Hills suggested a canal twenty-four feet wide and fifteen feet deep, with three sets of double locks, following a straighter route at the western end out the Manomet River into Buzzards Bay. He put the cost, including land and bridges, at £70,000 or about $350,000. A hefty tab, coming at a time when common laborers earned eight dollars per month and skilled masons were making fifteen dollars per month.

Still, the court went ahead and ordered a survey of marine traffic sailing around the cape. The results showed that one-half the vessels would continue using the outside route. That figure, along with the cost, dissuaded the legislature from building the canal. Significantly, though, it authorized anyone who wanted to build the waterway to do so and to charge tolls for its use.

The first person to exercise that option was a James Sullivan, who, with a number of others, petitioned the court in 1798 for rights to establish a private corporation to build and run a canal. The court permitted Sullivan to make surveys which, if found practicable, would be followed by rights of incorporation to be given at the next court session.

And in Sandwich, at a town meeting on May 14, 1801, citizens approved a petition from Thomas Parker Batcheller to build a waterway he said would be thirty-two feet wide with an adjacent towpath for horses of twelve feet. (At that time either the state or the Town of Sandwich could grant permission to build a canal, since the proposed route lay completely within town limits.)

The mood in Sandwich became one of optimism and enthusiasm—a minor outbreak of canal fever. Marvelous things were prophesied for the town: hundreds of new dwellings, better employment opportunities, higher real estate values, easier transportation of wood, and more warehouses. A boom in north-south trade was predicted that would, in the words of one resident, "confer immense advantages on the vicinity of such a channel of communication." But all the excitement turned out to be a false alarm—the efforts of both Sullivan and Batcheller came to nothing.

In the winter of 1803 the Massachusetts General Court came alive again to do what it did best—form a committee. This one, a joint committee, was charged with investigating four canal projects with the possibility of encouraging some of them. The plans singled out were: a waterway across Cape Cod from the sea on the south to the sea on the north; a waterway from Narragansett Bay through Taunton and the North River; a waterway from Millers River to the Nashua River in the western part of the state; and a waterway from Boston to Worcester, using either the Neponset or the Charles River. Nothing happened.

Nor did anything happen the following year, when the legislature granted permission to a group to hold a lottery to raise capital for a canal from Eastham to Orleans, across the central part of the cape. The group planned to use Boat Meadow Creek for much of the distance. But as this route would have lessened the distance and danger only slightly in comparison to an outside passage, the plan never inspired much interest. The Eastham-Orleans Canal Company managed to stay alive until 1817, when it secured a state charter to build a canal and charge vessels using it ten cents per ton. Shortly thereafter the company vanished.

In 1811 Thomas Batcheller was getting busy again in Sandwich. He and his associates had gotten permission from landowners to cut a canal along the valley of the isthmus, and they petitioned the legislature for a charter; their timing could not have been worse. The next year war broke out with Great Britain, squelching all canal plans. The British fleet, operating out of Provincetown, made it dangerous for Americans to even try to sail around Cape Cod during the War of 1812. Few did; instead, they returned to sailing up the Scusset or Manomet and portaging their boats between the rivers. It was rugged and slow—but safe.

There were no specific proposals for a Cape Cod canal for several years, but the war had underscored the value of such a waterway for defense, and word of the Erie Canal and success in building canals elsewhere spurred on local interest in Massachusetts. A special town meeting in Sandwich in January of 1818 saw a unanimous vote cast in favor of a petition to construct a canal by Israel Thorndike. Three weeks later, the legislature granted Thorndike a charter, permitting his Massachusetts Bay Canal Corporation to sell 10,000 shares of stock at fifty dollars per share. If that half-million dollars proved insufficient, the corporation was allowed to sell "any necessary number" of additional shares to pay for construction. The finished canal was to be large enough to handle vessels of ten-foot draft along a route between Buzzards Bay and Barnstable Bay, and for that route the charter permitted the taking of land 825 feet wide and provided jury trials to settle the rights of landowners who disputed damage awards. The charter also provided that bridges had to be built to span the canal and had to be maintained free; the project was to be finished in six years; and no taxes were to be due on the land until the canal produced income from the toll rates, set by the state at $0.30 to $1.50 per ton. These provisions, with the exception of the liberal clause providing for sales of additional shares if necessary, set a pattern for future charters.

The corporation wanted its own survey and hired Loammi Baldwin to do it. Working at top speed, he completed the survey in four days. He opted for a route that would use the Back River on the west, turn north to the Manomet and then east down the natural valley of the isthmus. According to Baldwin's estimate, a fifty-foot channel of sixteen-foot depth, with two storm locks, would cost almost 750 thousand dollars. Construction was not begun during the life of the charter, but this hardly surprised the growing number of skeptics. In 1824 a six-year extension was granted the Massachusetts Bay Canal Corporation.

Sometimes, during this arduous period of false starts, it seemed as though the reported obstacles were largely imaginary. Once a group of Boston businessmen formed a committee to investigate the feasibility of a Cape Cod canal. Their report was favorable, conceding that ships using such a waterway would save a considerable distance and escape "very formidable difficulties." They found just one problem—a strong current. That, they feared, might in time wash away the entire cape. Their efforts, like so many others, came to nothing.

On January 5, 1824, the scene shifted from local and state surveys to the federal government. Sen. James Lloyd of Massachusetts successfully introduced a resolution in the United States Senate asking the Committee on Roads and Canals to request the president to order a survey for a canal large enough for warships to sail between Buzzards Bay and Barnstable Bay.

Once before, in 1808, the federal government had shown interest in a Cape Cod canal, as Treasury Secretary Albert Gallatin led a national effort to improve transportation. Although his surveys helped other projects, Cape Cod did not benefit. Indeed, Gallatin was pessimistic about a cut through the isthmus, citing such drawbacks as differences in time and height of tides at either end of the proposed canal, shoals in Buzzards Bay, and lack of safe places to anchor at Sandwich. He did not like the Hyannis-Barnstable Harbor route either, as this left the shifting, dangerous shoals of Nantucket and Vineyard sounds to be navigated. Gallatin did, however, think there might be some merit to a proposed twenty-six-mile route from Boston Harbor to Narragansett Bay, using the Taunton River, but his interest was never pursued.

Now, in 1824, Lloyd's resolution produced a board of investigation, known as the Board of Internal Improvements, that partially affirmed Gallatin's opinions. The Hyannis-Barnstable Harbor route, it reported, should be dropped entirely, but it acknowledged there were advantages to the Boston Harbor-Narragansett Bay idea. In retrospect, that might have been a good route to follow up. The path was well protected, with a safe approach through Long Island Sound into the bay, and it would have given many landlocked towns access to the sea. On the other hand, though there were longer canals at the time, this one would have had to have been wider than most to accommodate coastal sailing vessels. Also, as builders of that time were limited to hand labor and black powder instead of the mechanical dredges that were to come, the board recommended more studies.

The panel differed sharply with Gallatin when it came to a cut through the isthmus, however. It was quite sanguine about that route, calling it practicable, a place where "nature has left little to do to unite the two bays." In the fall of 1824, the secretary of war ordered the Army Corps of Engineers to survey a route there. Maj. P. H. Perrault, one of its best topographical engineers, was assigned to the project. His detailed study came out in 1825, laying out a route through the Back River on the west and offering two outlets as alternatives on the east. It was a good report, but it remained in dry dock.

Ever hopeful, the residents of Sandwich asked their legislators to get the Massachusetts General Court to pass a resolution calling for the state's senators and congressmen to work toward obtaining federal aid for a canal across the cape. But this, too, was to no avail.

Three years after Perrault's survey, the Board of Internal Improvements thought that the prospect of a canal might be worth another visit to the cape and, of course, another survey. Cape Cod waited two more years for this report. Issued in February of 1830, it recommended an entrance to the canal at the Back River on the west and a tide lock with a lift of over twelve feet. The canal should be sixty feet wide on the surface and have a thirty-six-foot channel, eight feet deep. The suggested width for the towpath was nine feet. On the eastern end of the isthmus, the recommended entrance was one mile north of the Scusset River, to avoid the marshes. An eastern tidal lock with an eight-foot lift was suggested. Each lock was to be 107 feet long by 26 feet wide. The costs ranged from $455,000 to $704,000, depending on the way the canal was to be built.

That study met the same fate as so many of its predecessors—oblivion. By 1828, as Sen. S. W. McCall had described it a few years earlier, every grain of sand along the whole route had been made the victim of an algebraic equation. When the Massachusetts General Court held its opening session in May of 1830, Gov. Levi Lincoln ordered an end to the surveys. He merely asked the legislature to ponder the value of a Cape Cod canal and to decide if it would be worth appealing to the federal government to build one. But such an appeal would have been in vain. Andrew Jackson had assumed the presidency, and internal improvements financed by the treasury were not part of his plans. The surveys and reports were filed. Canal fever was on the wane throughout the rest of the country, and the project that had been the first proposed public work in the New World still had not left the drawing board.

Why, then, were papers being shuffled when everywhere else dirt was being shoveled? The answer is probably that the motivation for building other canals was primarily commercial, while the principal reason for a Cape Cod canal was humanitarian—to save lives. For example, in a series of articles in the *Commercial Gazette* of Boston in 1797, Thomas Wallcut expressed horror over the loss of life from ships wrecked while rounding the cape. He formed the Philanthropic Society, an organization dedicated to seeing that a Cape Cod canal was built, and urged members to keep statistics on lives, ships, and other property lost through cape marine disasters. To Wallcut, the prevention of these disasters would be an act "so humane, so patriotic, so religious" as to make the construction of a canal mandatory.

But the Commonwealth of Massachusetts never appeared overly impressed by these arguments. For the most part it left lifesaving efforts to the Massachusetts Humane Society, a private volunteer group organized along the lines of the present-day Red Cross. The federal government finally established rescue stations along the cape in the mid-1800s, with the state never having contributed more than a few dollars to Wallcut's mission of mercy.

As for commercial incentives, the Massachusetts government might have been more interested if more traffic on a canal was expected to be *within* the state, but that was not the case. Instead, the primary users would have been coastal ships, traveling from Boston to New York, Philadelphia, Baltimore, Virginia, South Carolina, and beyond.

For thirty years after 1830 the idea of a Cape Cod canal remained dormant. Glass manufacturing, started in 1825, brought prosperity to Sandwich. At the same time, railroads were introducing a new era of transportation to America. The iron rails were laid down the natural valley of the isthmus, and the first train arrived in Sandwich in 1848. From there people took stage coaches "down cape." Sandwich served as the railhead of the Cape Cod Central for six years until track reached Hyannis in 1854, Wellfleet in 1869, and Provincetown in 1873. Unlike canal fever, which brought only surveys, railroad fever brought a new means of transportation to the isolated cape.

Ironically, though, while railroads killed off much healthier canal projects elsewhere, they were not a severe threat to the proposed Cape Cod Canal. New England's tradition was one of ships, and its many rivers meant that railways would sometimes need bridges every few miles. Also, coastal vessels were usually quicker than trains, and they specialized in high-volume cargo—particularly coal—which the rail lines would just as soon have eschewed in favor of lower volume goods, which drew higher rates. There still was hope.

It was not until the year 1860 that the Cape Cod Canal project was re-exhumed, this time in a manner calculated to get a meaningful response. Speaking at his Inaugural in January, Massachusetts Gov. Nathaniel Banks referred to the many surveys made from which so little remained. Banks stressed the fact that so much information had been lost; he asked that the remaining material be taken better care of.

The legislature responded with a committee—specifically a joint special committee that two months later brought in a traffic report indicating that 120 ships rounded the cape daily and that these ships were larger on the average than those rounding the cape when the last survey had been made. Consequently any proposed canal would have to be deeper than earlier plans had suggested—sixteen to eighteen feet at least. The report also suggested that the Back River with its deep harbor be incorporated in the route of the canal rather than dredging a channel from Buzzards Bay into the Monument River. The committee reported that a canal with harbors to serve the coastal trade could be built for $1.25 million.

Naturally, further studies were suggested, and another committee—a Joint Recess Committee—was formed. As a fact-finding committee, it had power to hire engineers and other experts to gather data on costs, routes, and methods of construction, and to report back to the legislature. Two years and ten thousand dollars later the report was finished, declaring that "the matter has now been fully investigated; all that modern science can determine has been revealed." The committee indicatd its lack of interest in seeing the state build the canal, noting that if the canal were ever to be built, federal help would be necessary. It ducked the issue of practicality, leaving it to "those interested in the proposed improvement [who] may decide upon the practical value of the work, and to what extent the state shall aid in the enterprise." A business group from Boston canvassed mercantile and shipping interests to see who might use such a waterway and what savings might result, coming up with an annual sum of just over $1 million. The committee, however, did do something of importance: all material on the proposed canal was put in one package.

The Joint Recess Committee persuaded three federal officials, all with either canal or nautical experience, to study the canal: Gen. Joseph Totten, of the Army Corps of Engineers; Prof. A. D. Bache, superintendent of the Coast and Geodetic Survey, and Comdr. Charles Davis of the United States Navy. They studied the material available and walked over the proposed route of the canal through the isthmus. Their conclusions raised the hopes of canal proponents. A canal, they said, would be easy and relatively inexpensive to build, partly because land that was not being used could be purchased cheaply. And a big harbor with a causeway connecting the islands in Buzzards Bay (Hog, Mashnee and Tobys) should be created.

One of their suggestions, to hire a good engineer, was adopted. He was George R. Baldwin (the son of Loammi Baldwin), who, after surveying the isthmus and reading the legislative file of past studies, including traffic surveys, decided to "make a canal large enough for the biggest coastal boats—those of the Fall River Line." His specifications: a canal with a surface width of 240 feet, a channel of 120 feet, and a depth of 18 feet. At the eastern end of the canal, near Sandwich, two routes were planned. If the canal with the more northerly entrance (which would avoid marshes) was built, Baldwin estimated the cost to be $9.914 million; for the more southerly entrance, at Sagamore, the figure was $9.557 million. The legislative committee winced at those prices and looked for ways to cut them. They believed the elimination of locks would save money, but their alternative, a twenty-mile, winding canal to reduce the velocity of the current, was, to say the least, foolish. Since the isthmus was eight miles long by way of the valley, just where those twenty miles of canal were to go was never made clear.

While conducting his survey, Baldwin made test borings of the subsurface and found gravel, clay, and sand. He erroneously concluded—he was not alone in this respect—that "large boulders along the route were superficial and would never be a problem." His error mattered little, for neither the state nor the federal government did anything with Baldwin's report besides file it.

In 1870, a group headed by one Alpheus Hardy, calling itself the Cape Cod Ship Canal Company, was granted a charter to dig a canal through the isthmus. Work was to start within two years and was to be completed within seven. The company was required to pay for any damages to the herring fish industry in addition to assuming the regular responsibilities of constructing free bridges and operating free ferries, relocating railroads and roads, and paying land damages that had become standard in all charters. The right to issue up to $10 million worth of stock at $100 per share was also granted, as was the right to issue construction bonds. Land could be taken up to one thousand feet in width for the right-of-way, on which no taxes would be due until two years after the canal was in operation.

The legislature called on the federal government to build the breakwater on the eastern end of the canal, and Washington appeared interested enough to send Col. J. G. Foster to survey the isthmus. Foster suggested a free canal without locks, but recommended guard gates for use during extra high tides. His proposal called for a channel larger than Baldwin's: 300 feet on the surface, 198 feet in the channel, and 23 feet in depth. Even though Foster's proposed canal required removing more than 18 million cubic yards of earth and debris than Baldwin's, Foster thought the canal could be built within three years.

To protect its eastern entrance, Foster suggested a 4,000-foot breakwater parallel to shore to be built at a cost of $2 million. In his report, he cited the toll of the previous ten years, during which 617 ships had been wrecked while rounding the cape with a known loss of sixty-seven lives, in addition to seven wrecks with a loss of lives whose total was unknown. Foster concluded that a canal would have military value in war at least equal to that of its commercial value in peacetime.

On April 2, 1870, the Massachusetts legislature passed a resolution calling on the United States Congress to grant an appropriation to build a breakwater at the eastern end of the proposed canal; this would also create a harbor of refuge. As a United States Senate Joint Resolution it was reported out of the Committee on Commerce on June 16 by Sen. Zachariah Chandler of Michigan, who had a considerable interest in legislation involving shipping and maritime affairs. But like many a ship unprotected by the breakwater it sought to provide, the bill foundered.

Yet another engineer who surveyed the isthmus, in 1871, was Joseph P. Frizell. He saw no need for locks; in fact, he thought the free canal with a good current would handle the problem of dredging by scouring the channel. Frizell cited part of the Clyde River at Glasgow as an example of a waterway whose channel was maintained by scouring. So it would be at Cape Cod, he believed. He was wrong. But it was to be many years until anyone would find that out.

Although the Cape Cod Ship Canal Company did no work on the waterway, it applied for extensions of its charter, which were routinely granted in 1872, 1875, and 1876.

It was during the 1870s that one of the country's most famous civil engineers came to Cape Cod to study the possibility of a canal. He was Clemens Herschel, former president of the American Society of Civil Engineers. Herschel thought that locks were unnecessary and would, in fact, hinder navigation through the proposed canal. The canal he suggested was rather modest in size and cost, yet, he felt, could handle 95 percent of the traffic rounding the cape. For $2 million, according to Herschel, a 65-foot channel of 18-foot depth could be built with a water surface of 110 to 134 feet. His traffic estimate of 4 million cargo tons per year with tolls of ten to fifteen cents per ton would pay the $100,000-per-year maintenance costs. The legislative committee, impressed by Herschel's report and the fact that his thinking with regard to locks coincided with that of Foster and Frizell, decided locks would not be necessary. It was a wise move, for locks would have cut down the number of vessels that could pass through the canal, and elimination of the current would also have meant the canal would freeze over during bad cold spells.

By the end of the 1870s the Cape Cod Ship Canal Company, which had held a charter for the full decade, had built nothing. The next person to propose building the canal was Henry M. Whitney, a Boston businessman and head of the Metropolitan Steamship Company. His application for a charter was cause for optimism, as his enterprises were awash with success. In April of 1880, the legislature granted a charter to Whitney's Cape Cod Canal Company that would become effective on November 1 unless the Cape Cod Ship Canal Company had spent $100,000 on construction by that time. If the Cape Cod Ship Canal Company did not meet that deadline it would have to turn over all its land and materials to Whitney, without compensation. An ominous threat!

Still, the Ship Canal Company managed to watch the good construction months of summer slip by, finally moving on September 15. At a spot called Town Neck, about one-half mile from the beach in Sandwich, a work force of 112 Italian laborers from New York started swinging shovels and picks after one James Keenan dug a ceremonial wheelbarrow full of sand at 7 A.M. that day. Within two weeks there were at least 400—some say 500—Italians at work, and the tiny wooden wheelbarrows were replaced by larger tip carts.

The laborers lived in tents near the work site, an area that was actually some distance south of the routes proposed for the canal. The site apparently was chosen simply to give the impression that the company was at last doing something and thus entitled to keep its charter.

But the Italians were not paid, and when food ran out they became bitter. In a sullen mood, they marched on the company's office in Sandwich on October 13 and captured—if that is the word—the son of the contractor with the idea of holding him to force his father to produce their pay. The single interpreter managed to out-shout the angry laborers, convincing them their ransom idea was not so good. They released the relieved young man and returned to their tents near the ditch they had worked so hard to dig. Singly and in small groups they roamed through the town of Sandwich, seeking food in exchange for odd jobs. They were a pathetic group—unable to speak English, strangers in an alien land, viewed with suspicion, hungry, frustrated, victimized, and powerless.

Several politicians called the episode "the Neapolitan revolt," and maintained that "Sandwich was for a week under arms." This is mostly nonsense, although there are those today who believe such tales. At all events, the selectmen wired the governor for reinforcements and some state police were sent, augmented by patrols of local deputies. The Town of Sandwich fed the Italians and arranged through a state agency to return them by train to New York City in groups of sixty per day. By November 1 they were gone, and the sorriest episode in the story of the Cape Cod Canal was over. Massachusetts paid the Town of Sandwich twenty-five dollars for food for the laborers, but refused a bill for $205 for "special police expenses." The weekly, the *Yarmouth Register*, referring to the Italians, editorialized: "they have, all things considered, acted full as well, if not better, than the same number of Yankees or Irish would have done."

The abortive effort by the Cape Cod Ship Canal Company left the door open for Whitney and his group; they stepped in tentatively. Whitney's effort was one of fact-finding and his engineers brought transits and equipment to make test borings. He emphasized that he was unwilling to spend $10 or $12 million on a canal.

With political clout in Boston, Whitney had no difficulty getting the legislature to grant a one year's extension for filing construction plans.

And for the first time since Colonel Foster had been sent to the cape in 1870, the federal government seemed interestd in the building of a canal across Cape Cod. On March 3, 1881, the first session of the forty-seventh Congress appropriated $1,000 for an investigation of the feasibility of building a canal as part of the Rivers and Harbor Act. This paid for Lt. Col. G. K. Warren, of the Army Corps of Engineers, to go to the cape where he promptly established a good working relationship with Whitney's engineers. While Warren surveyed the upper parts of Buzzards Bay, Whitney's men conducted a series of test borings there and at the eastern end of the proposed canal.

Warren figured costs on approach channels and a breakwater and asked for money to begin the work. He felt an entry through Buzzards Bay of 500-foot width and twenty-one-foot depth would cost $350 thousand. Although hard clay turned up in the borings, Warren estimated $918 thousand as the cost of a channel to the beach at the eastern entrance and a pair of jetties to protect the entrance. The estimates represented reasonable figures, but after an engineer brought the pessimistic news that he had discovered quicksand, Whitney quit. Had he known what others would later discover, that the quicksand deposits were small and inconsequential, Whitney probably would be remembered today as the father of the Cape Cod Canal. Instead, his name has sunk in the mire of other unfulfilled dreams.

With things at a standstill, a New Englander made a suggestion that found a warm reception at the White House. After Secretary of the Navy William E. Chandler, of New Hampshire, suggested that a canal across Cape Cod would help the nation's defenses, Pres. Chester A. Arthur recommended its inclusion in a system of coastal waterways. A congressional committee on railways and canals reported favorably on a bill that included Colonel Warren's proposals, including the view that the federal government should help pay for a breakwater and harbor at the eastern end of the canal. Congress did not pass the bill, however.

With Whitney out of the picture, two other groups filed for a charter. The winner, in June of 1883, was the Cape Cod Ship Canal Company, a new concern with an old name. Its leaders were William Seward, Jr., Samuel Fessenden of Sandwich, Alfred D. Fox, and George H. Titcomb, who had been prominent in the former Cape Cod Ship Canal Company—the one that brought in the Italian laborers in the fall of 1880. That did not weigh against him, however. Perhaps he was contrite.

Because Fox, who was from Montreal, alleged he had superior lines to near-limitless quantities of Canadian money, the others agreed he should get the contract to do the actual building. Within two weeks, Fox granted the subcontract to Frederick A. Lockwood, a manufacturer of marine hoisting equipment on the East Boston waterfront. The Canadian money went elsewhere and without it the other directors dropped Fox as a partner; in October they signed a contract with Lockwood to dig the canal.

Since one provision of its charter, to spend $25,000 within four months, had not been met, the company decided to build a dock for use along the as yet nonexistent canal. The directors chose a spot in Sandwich on dry land

and brought in oak piles via Railway Express, an extravagant manner of shipment calculated to spend money rapidly. The dock was put together hastily, the company showed receipts totaling $40,000, and the charter was kept alive.

Lockwood soon emerged as a major figure in the new company (though legally he remained a subcontractor), having obtained rights to a new dredge designed by a Californian named John A. Ball. Lockwood built the machinery at his East Boston plant and assembled his dredge for $75,000. It used an endless chain of thirty-nine metal buckets to pick up material and raise it fifty-six feet to a hopper, where water forced it out through pipes to the canal banks. After a conventional dredge cut a channel through the beach, two tugboats brought Lockwood's machine to Sandwich where it entered the small cut to begin work. Large crowds poured onto Scusset Beach to cheer the day the dredge arrived. The Cape Cod Canal had begun at last.

The work site was a popular place for local residents, who came to picnic and to watch the dredge on its westward trek. Powered by two seventy-five-horsepower steam engines, it hissed and clanked its way through the marshes, digging a canal over 100 feet wide and 15 feet deep. It broke down frequently but the crowds were happy just commenting on the repair work, which Lockwood performed personally. The dredge's captain was well known in Sandwich. Indeed, Cornelius Driscoll had become a local hero when he helped fishermen reach shore after their ships had been trapped by ice in Cape Cod Bay during an especially bitter spell in 1873. After the dredge ceased operations for lack of money, Driscoll was kept on as a watchman for a few years.

Money was a problem. Lockwood claimed to have invested $150,000 of his own funds, but he did not have nearly enough money of his own to spend it the way he did. Instead, most of the backing, including the $200,000 deposit, came from copper mines through a Boston businessman named Quincy Adams Shaw. (Shaw was never active in the canal company, preferring to have his interests managed by Thomas L. Livermore.) It is also believed Charles C. Dodge of the Phelps-Dodge Copper Corporation contributed a substantial amount. The finance situation was further tangled when Lockwood took an option on 50,000 shares of stock at fifty cents each, a move he claimed gave him voting rights on those shares, and one that cost the other directors—Seward, Fox, and Fessenden—their control of the company. They did not go quietly; instead, in an effort to regain control, they waged legal fights for a decade—fights that led to a number of hearings by legislative committees and that weakened the concern.

In the midst of all this a four-year extension of Lockwood's charter was granted in 1887. But two years later, after his East Boston plant burned down, he became seriously ill. In 1890 Quincy Adams Shaw took over what little was left of Lockwood's interest in the Cape Cod Ship Canal Company —namely, the ditch, the dredge, and the title to land acquired. The bucket dredge ran for a few months, until June of that year, when Shaw's money lost steam. Then it was sold and the machinery removed. The dredge was not a reliable machine, but it had cut a canal about 7,000 feet long, even though the first 1,500 feet from the beach west had filled up with sand. The steam generator and electric lighting system—the first on Cape Cod—provided illumination for a social event at the 250th Anniversary of Sandwich.

In 1891, when the charter that Shaw now held was to run out, Thomas Livermore represented him in testifying for an extension. Alfred Fox also sought the charter, repeating that old story about his Canadian money sources. But the legislature required both a half-million-dollar deposit as proof of performance and liability for the bonds Lockwood issued as collateral for loans. That deposit would become a major stumbling block to those who hoped to build a canal in years to come. Evidently Shaw had had enough and Fox could not tap the Canadian cash he so often referred to; although he actually obtained a charter, it lapsed three months later when he failed to produce the deposit.

The next year, 1892, began a minor flood of applications from groups who believed themselves eminently qualified to build a Cape Cod canal if only given the opportunity. Seven petitions came in that year, eight in 1895, seven in 1898, six in 1899, and a few others were thrown in for good measure. Many of the groups asked for help from the state or federal government, but it never came through, and they remained stymied by the $500,000 deposit.

Quincy Adams Shaw began the rush, even though a year before he had failed to come up with the deposit. He had Livermore try to obtain a charter to revive the Cape Cod Ship Canal Company, bringing in Lockwood to testify on behalf of the petition. Shaw had one major factor in his favor: he owned about one thousand acres of land that Lockwood had acquired in the 1880s for $69,000, then sold to him in 1890. Even so, that effort failed.

From 1884 to 1906 there was periodic interest in a canal route using the Bass River. The idea was to enter the river at Yarmouth on Nantucket Sound, then follow a series of tidal creeks and ponds more than halfway across the cape. There an extensive land cut would be necessary. The northern entrance would be at Barnstable Harbor, from which a tidal creek flowed inland. But this Bass River route would not avoid the shoals of Nantucket Sound and would present other drawbacks: the tidal current would be strong and cutting through the high ground would be a formidable task. The only charter ever granted for the proposed route went in 1895 to the Massachusetts Ship Canal Company, which failed to raise the deposit. Except for occasional dredging to maintain a modest channel for yachts and fishing boats, no work was ever done on Bass River.

In 1896, the Massachusetts Maritime Canal Company received a charter, but it was allowed to lapse like so many others. And finally, in 1898, Gov. Roger Wolcott sponsored a bill to dig a Cape Cod canal using convicts as the labor force. Although supported by the citizens of Sandwich, the bill died. By then local residents were becoming rather cynical about the whole affair. The editor of the *Barnstable Patriot* wrote: "No less than seven projects for a Cape Cod Canal are to come before the legislature this year. Meanwhile, despite all threats, the Cape hangs on to the mainland with the grim determination characteristic of its people."

Then, with but seven months left in the nineteenth century, the charter was granted (after some hefty lobbying) under which the Cape Cod Canal would be built. There were nine names on the petition for the Boston, Cape Cod and New York Canal Company, but only one would be a factor—DeWitt Clinton Flanagan. Flanagan's grandfather had been a friend of DeWitt Clinton, and the grandson's first and middle names seemed enough to produce success, recalling the glories of the Erie Canal and the New York governor who was its principal political benefactor. Flanagan's money came from beer, a family enterprise with no connection to the construction or maritime industries. However, like Frederick Lockwood, Flanagan did have some money in a patent for a dredge and hoped that a fleet of such machines would produce revenue during the construction of the canal.

The charter's provisions were similar to those of its predecessors. The cash deposit, however, was to be $200,000, and the Commission on Harbor and Public Land specified minimum dimensions for the waterway: a 25-foot deep channel, 100 feet wide, with a surface of 200 feet.

The Boston, Cape Cod and New York Canal Company was allowed to raise $12 million, one-half through the sale of stock and the other half through the sale of fifty-year, 6 percent bonds, both to be issued only to cover actual expenditures. Tolls were left to the company, which was also given the right of eminent domain. Landowners had their damage claims judged by the county commissioners, but the claims could be appealed through a jury trial in Barnstable County Court.

In his search for money, Flanagan persuaded a Baltimore bank, the Maryland Trust Company, to handle the financing. Its representative, Col. Alfred L. Rives, acting as consulting engineer, drew up plans with Elmer L. Corthell, who three years earlier had organized the Massachusetts Maritime Canal Company. Rives had been in Panama as superintendent of the Panama Railroad. The two engineers planned a canal with a straight approach up the middle of Buzzards Bay—from Wings Neck past Hog Island and through the upper bay into the mouth of the Monument River. This approach, ultimately dug by the Army Corps of Engineers in the 1930s, is the one used today. They did not want locks, anticipating at most a four-mile-per-hour current, and one of their best suggestions was to dig "in the dry," using steam shovels through the middle of the land cut.

Flanagan was forced to go elsewhere for capital when the Maryland Trust Company backed out. Although anxious to start construction, he was not forced to resort to the frenzied activity of previous companies within a certain period of time to keep his charter. Construction had to begin three months after plans to relocate the Old Colony Railroad were approved by the Joint Board. (The Commonwealth of Massachusetts had created a joint board from the two agencies that regulated waterways, public land, and the railroads: the Commission on Harbor and Public Land and the Board of Railroad Commissioners.) Flanagan managed to delay the relocation plans of the railroad and, therefore, was able to take his time finding a financial backer.

Five years after Flanagan received the charter, he found the man who would build the Cape Cod Canal—although at first neither Flanagan nor the man himself knew this.

2

Let's Build A Canal

AUGUST Perry Belmont was the son of August Belmont, a famous private banker and financier. The father had come to the United States from Europe in 1837, following financial training with the banking firm of the Rothschilds. He later worked closely with J. P. Morgan and twice was part of a syndicate that floated major bond issues for the federal government.

His marriage to Caroline Slidell Perry also wed the family to Cape Cod and the sea: the Perry family came from Bourne; its members sailed the world. Caroline's father, Comdr. Matthew Calbraith Perry, led "the opening of Japan" to American trade and influence. In 1853 in Tokyo Bay and the next year at Yokahama, Perry brought battleships and other blessings of Western civilization to the unenlightened East. The commodore's brother, Capt. Oliver Hazard Perry, entered American history as the hero of the Battle of Lake Erie; after sinking a British fleet there in 1813, he proclaimed: "We have met the enemy, and they are ours."

August Perry Belmont was born to this imposing heritage in 1853. As a teenager he attended Harvard College; a classmate and friend was Theodore Roosevelt, who would become known as the president who built the Panama Canal. While a member of the college track team, Belmont had a local shoemaker add spikes to his running shoes—equipment that later became standard for track and field events and that the banker's son is usually credited with originating.

After graduating Belmont entered his father's banking house, August Belmont and Company. The family business prospered and Belmont became its president after his father died in 1890. The house specialized in railroad bonds, leading Belmont to a deep interest in and knowledge of transportation. For a while he was board chairman of the Louisville and Nashville Railroad, and his private car, the Mineola, was known to railroad crews on most American lines.

Appalled by accidents and the lack of safety devices in some industries, Belmont pushed for a workman's compensation law in New York State through his membership in the National Civic Federation. Success was slow, but it came eventually. His fascination with new things extended to the young aviation industry, which he aided when it needed it most. He was a director of the Wright Company, which manufactured airplanes, and helped finance a French concern experimenting with airplane stabilizers. But even though he was a capitalist and a friend to many capitalists, his was not the party of privilege—in politics, Belmont was a Democrat.

Belmont's youthful interests in sports also expanded with the power, prestige, and wealth of his career. He bred thoroughbreds—the most notable of which was Man O' War—built Belmont Park, founded the American Kennel Club, and twice helped build yachts that defended America's Cup against British challengers. After the victory of his second ship, he said privately that he "had rooted for the English sailors, believing it to be in the best interest of the sport." He was a director of both the Metropolitan Opera and the Metropolitan Museum of Art.

Belmont loved a challenge. In New York City, trolley lines, which cluttered the streets, were replaced by elevated trains after 1895. But "els" used a lot of space, and in rapid transit circles the talk of the future was subways. The idea was not new. Yet in the country's largest city no one came forward with the combination of drive and money to build one. No one, that is, until August Perry Belmont. He planned and built a subway line, "The Fourth Avenue," which opened in 1904 and at first ran only from Fourteenth to Thirty-Fourth Streets.

The engineer in charge of the subway project had an international reputation for success. William Barclay Parsons was a builder of railroads in the United States and China. A civil engineer by training and profession, he was a member of an old New York family and had written books on engineering as a theoretical and applied science. Unlike many in his field, he had a superior command of the language, both spoken and written. His library was huge, his reading interests broad—and he absorbed what he read.

While others carried on the subway work, Parsons sought new challenges and went to Panama in 1904 as a highly respected member of the commission gathered to plan the cut through Central America to link the Atlantic and Pacific oceans. Parsons thought a sea-level canal without locks was best for Panama, while the Army Corps of Engineers wanted a canal with locks. The army got its way, despite Parsons and a majority of commission votes to the contrary. Parsons returned to the United States in 1905.

When Belmont, the financier, and Parsons, the visionary engineer, had made their plans for the subway, they agreed on a contractor to build it: Michael J. Degnon of New York City. Having developed a close working relationship during that pioneer effort, the three would again join forces to build where others had talked, planned, and failed.

DeWitt Clinton Flanagan approached Belmont with the idea of building a canal across Cape Cod in 1904, when the latter's banking firm and the banker himself were at the pinnacle of prosperity and prestige. Flanagan's direct approach and knowledge of routes and potential for the canal interested Belmont. They met many times, with Flanagan repeatedly stressing a canal's value: the safer passage would mean lower insurance rates for shippers, the time saved in using the short cut would mean more trips and greater income for ship owners, and shipping rates would in turn be lowered. How could a toll canal with all those positive features fail to turn a profit? Flanagan produced the 1899 traffic survey by Rives and Corthell, the engineers for his venture with the Maryland Trust Company. They had figured annual cargo around the cape at 23,400,000 tons. An eight cent per ton toll would produce a little under $2 million in revenue. They figured a canal would pull an additional $750,000 away from the New York, New Haven and Hartford Railroad's Fall River Line. Passenger and freight business on that line used a water route between New York and Fall River, Newport, Providence, and New Bedford, and a rail line from those ports to Boston. With the canal the engineers envisioned, this freight, or a good portion of it, would be shipped entirely by water. The value of a canal across Cape Cod to the national defense was another point in favor of such a project: the navy could speed its coastal vessels through such a waterway in time of emergency. In suggesting the last point, perhaps a foray into the national treasury was in the back of Flanagan's mind.

It was all persuasive, but Belmont wanted to be sure. So he assigned two men to study the possibilities of a route across the cape and its potential traffic—Parsons, who functioned as chief engineer, and C. S. Sims, an authority on maritime traffic who reported on potential users and income.

Parsons arrived on the cape in February of 1906 and went to see Charles M. Thompson, who had been assistant engineer for Frederick Lockwood's effort. Thompson had remained in Sandwich with later companies until Flanagan hired him as resident engineer to select a route, determine the subsoil through test borings, and make tidal studies to gauge the current through a canal. Thompson supervised those efforts, adding data to his growing file, until 1903. When Belmont seemed interested in building the canal in 1906, Flanagan had Thompson go back to work. Thompson showed all his studies to Parsons, who went over the route down the isthmus and saw nothing that looked formidable; the two agreed that the canal would not be a difficult thing to build.

But at this juncture Belmont's chief engineer saw some test borings that seemed to contain quicksand. If that was the case, Parsons would advise against building. Thompson, who had been in the area for more than twenty years and knew it better than anyone, argued that the minute sand particles only turned up in borings from the deepest part of the isthmus. "They had sifted down through centuries," Thompson said, "a sort of natural settling only in that one area and are not true quicksand at all." That seemed a reasonable explanation to Parsons, but he ordered some more borings. After seeing the samples, he agreed: there was no quicksand.

Parsons wanted an open sea-level canal without locks; the current would scour the channel, he thought, reducing maintenance. Because the discovery of numerous boulders in the Buzzards Bay shallows promised difficult dredging and much blasting to remove them, he designed a channel with two turns that followed the contour of the shore—inside Mashnee Island and through Phinneys Harbor, with its entrance off Wings Neck.

Parsons hired Henry Welles Durham, a friend who had been working on the Panama Canal, as resident engineer to replace Thompson, who became real estate agent in charge of acquiring the remaining land. Durham, whose wife did not take kindly to Panama's climate, looked forward to the opportunity of working with his friend, as well as to the more hospitable weather. The new Panama recruit in turn hired two former Panama engineers to be in charge of the east and west divisions, C. T. Waring and A. S. Ackerman.

In the meantime, Sims had returned his traffic report to Belmont. Sims figured total tonnage around the cape at 27,400,000 per year in some 30,000 vessels. That figure did not include ships of deeper draft that went south of Nantucket Lightship; they would be unable to use a twenty-five-foot deep canal. Assuming only one-half the vessels would utilize the canal, paying four cents toll on each ton, Sims estimated annual income at $490 thousand. But, he wrote, three out of four ships would use the canal, producing a profit— after interest on the bonds, and maintenance and operating expenses—of $285 thousand to $373 thousand. Sims's conclusion: A Cape Cod canal "will be handsomely self-supporting" and its construction should begin.

While Belmont was collecting this technical information, Flanagan kept up the pressure on him. Flanagan wanted to divest himself of any direct control of a canal while keeping a large financial interest in it. The capitalist (as his occupation would be listed in a later canal prospectus) sought $500,000 in bonds and $2.4 million in stock for his holdings in the Boston, Cape Cod and New York Canal Company, which included the franchise and land to which he had acquired title or the option to purchase. He had bought 78 acres outright, while negotiating an option with Thomas L. Livermore, the front man for Quincy Adams Shaw, to buy Shaw's 1,002 acres. To build the canal, fewer than 500 additional acres would need to be acquired. Belmont and Flanagan reached agreement several times in 1906 and 1907, but the panic of 1907 caused them to postpone their plans. Under the final terms, achieved in 1907, Flanagan received $200,000 for the deposit he had made with the Commonwealth of Massachusetts, and $250,000 in canal bonds and $1.4 million in stock. Belmont received the franchise, the land, and the options.

With favorable reports from both his experts, Belmont moved ahead. But the technical reports were not all that impelled Belmont to build the canal. Just as building the New York City subway about which so many others had talked but done nothing was a challenge, so building the canal, which had produced lots of plans but no results, was a similar enterprise. Belmont also envisioned the canal as a memorial to his maternal ancestors, the Perrys of Cape Cod, for he was a sentimental man. What better tribute to a family of sailors than a canal crossing their estate at Bourne? Besides, Sims had said a canal would make money, and that is what successful banking is all about.

Little was standing in the banker's way. Past opposition to the canal by the New York, New Haven and Hartford Railroad (known as the New Haven Railroad) had vanished, probably for two reasons. First, the railroad's main line was operating at capacity, and a canal would attract bulk freight—mostly coal—moving by long, efficient tows, which rapidly were squeezing out schooners in the coastal trade. The railroad did not care about such low-paying traffic, preferring to move high-class freight, which paid better tariffs. The second factor was Belmont's friendship with J. P. Morgan, who controlled the New Haven. To Belmont, Morgan was "Jack."

Belmont opened New York and Boston offices of the Boston, Cape Cod and New York Canal Company, a Massachusetts corporation. For tax purposes a second company, the Cape Cod Construction Company, also with Belmont as president, was incorporated in Maine. It would own no equipment, borrow none, and buy none. Instead, all the actual building was subcontracted to concerns that furnished the plant.

From the Boston, Cape Cod and New York Canal Company's office on Tremont Street in Boston, an invitation was issued on February 6, 1907, to contractors who might wish to bid on the job. Written bids would be received until noon on March 28. A $75,000 certified check was required with the bid, to be applied toward the mandatory $750,000 performance bond. The Canal Company and the Joint Board agreed to award the contract to the firm with the lowest "satisfactory bid" for the whole project, including buying the remaining land, digging the canal and approach channels, relocating the railroad tracks, building breakwaters, highways, wharves, and bridges, and placing a layer of rough stone—riprap—along the water line to prevent erosion. Labor and materials were to be supplied by the contractor.

On March 27, 1907, Belmont's Cape Cod Construction Company submitted a bid of $11,990,000, to be paid as $6 million in bonds from Belmont's Boston, Cape Cod and New York Canal Company and the remainder in Canal Company stock. There was one other bid; it was rejected, because the firm, Holbrook, Cabot and Rollins, bid on parts of the job. The Construction Company and the Canal Company signed their contract on the same day the Construction Company's bid was submitted, rather than the following day, which had been announced as the deadline.

The Massachusetts Joint Board approved the plans and the contract on June 3. At the same time, with Flanagan working behind the scenes, the railroad commissioners on the board miraculously approved plans for relocating the tracks of the Old Colony Railroad down the isthmus. Under the formula of the 1899 Cape Cod Canal charter the company had ninety days in which to begin work.

Under the agreement, the Construction Company received working capital by selling $1 million in stock to members of a syndicate Belmont had organized. Syndicate members also agreed to subscribe to Canal Company bonds at 95 percent of par value, receiving the same amount of Canal Company stock for free. As work progressed, Construction Company engineers made monthly pilgrimmages to the Joint Board with estimates of the value of the work completed. When these were certified a Boston bank—the Old Colony Trust Company, trustee of the canal property through an arrangement with Belmont—sent Belmont that value in bonds and the same amount in stock, which was used to pay off the Construction Company or was sold to syndicate members to provide capital. The bonds, which were to pay 5 percent interest in two annual installments from January of 1910 to January of 1960, were sold only to friends of Belmont or of other syndicate members; stock went to the same subscribers as a bonus. Belmont never made any effort to sell either of the securities to the public.

On August 19, Chief Engineer Parsons dug a shovelful of sand from the canal route near Sagamore Village. Charles Thompson was in charge of about 100 laborers from Boston, who moved in with picks and shovels, loading the material on flat cars for a short trip to the Keith Car and Manufacturing Company, which needed fill at its Sagamore plant. Durham arrived a couple of weeks later as resident engineer; Thompson became the real estate agent; and the workers kept on shoveling, managing to complete 350 feet of the ditch. Then cold weather moved in, freezing canal work but doubtless pleasing Durham's wife. From their old house in Sandwich he wrote, "After three years of tropical heat, we could barely keep warm with a coal stove and an old-fashioned kitchen stove in front of which water froze on our cook's apron." The work did not amount to a thing, but it met the charter's requirement of work within ninety days. A legal beginning, though minor.

Thompson tried to be fair with his offers to purchase the remaining land the project needed. He had lived in Sandwich since the 1880s and knew both the people and their land well. Wearing unpressed suits and a straw hat in the summer, he was short and had an enormous stomach—a figure easily recognizable even at some distance. Evidently the visibility paid off in trust; Thompson bought two-thirds of the necessary land outright. If the owners did not agree to sell at the price he offered, the Construction Company took the matter to the Barnstable County Commissioners for settlement. If still unhappy, the owners had a final recourse to a jury trial in civil court. Only about 15 percent of the cases made it that far.

The county commissioners were entitled to $6 per day, for up to fifty days per year, for working on canal business. Since $300 was a nice sum in those days, the commissioners always put in for it, claiming to have earned it. Dr. William J. Reid quoted Durham as having said, "If one of the commissioners was sick, he still claimed the fee on the grounds he was lying here (in bed) thinking about the canal." But while some land owners muttered that the extravagant fees swayed the commissioners' verdict, most agreed they got a fair price. A notable exception was Mrs. Grover Cleveland, the widow of late President Cleveland. Mrs. Cleveland went to court to raise her claim for Gray Gables from $50,000 to $75,000, but company lawyers produced the original claim on which the president had done just the opposite, scribbled out $75,000 and wrote in $50,000. Mrs. Cleveland explained that the president had thought the $75,000 figure excessive. The verdict returned, however, was for a paltry $12,000. A friend of the Canal Company had been on the jury.

On May 15, 1909, the Construction Company signed a contract with the Degnon Cape Cod Canal Construction Company, an organization owned jointly by Degnon's New York firm, of subway fame, the Degnon Contracting Company, and the Furst-Clark Contracting Company of Baltimore and Galveston. This joint firm then subcontracted with the Degnon Contracting Company for the breakwater and riprap and with Furst-Clark for the actual excavation of the canal.

The first sign of construction was the arrival of the two-masted schooner *Annie F. Lewis* with granite from quarries at Blue Hill, Maine. With sails furled and the tugboat *Mary Arnold* alongside, the *Lewis* dropped anchor one-half mile off Scusset Beach on June 19, transferring her granite to the deck of a steam lighter. The lighter, a flat scow with hoisting equipment built onto the deck, had been towed that day to a position some fifteen hundred feet from the beach, the center of the proposed 3,000-foot breakwater. When later ships arrived building could proceed in both directions simultaneously. The lighter positioned, two black deck hands fastened a heavy pair of steel tongs onto the first block. A steam winch hissed and clanked and the block cleared the deck, the boom carrying it up and over the side. Seconds later came a great splash as the first block of granite sank in forty feet of water. Countless tons remained to be sunk before the breakwater would rise eight feet above high tide, solidly stopping waves from the fierce storms that come across Cape Cod Bay.

On June 22, three days after the breakwater began, William Barclay Parsons dug a shovelful of earth near Bournedale. It is not recorded whether August Perry Belmont knew that his chief engineer had beaten him to it, but that afternoon at exactly 1:20 P.M., Belmont, using a sterling silver shovel that Michael Degnon had bought for him at Tiffany's, dug a little dirt and moved it a few feet. About fifty investors, company directors, railroad executives, politicians, and relatives were on hand. The day was one for ceremony, and the spot selected—the home of Belmont's maternal ancestors, the Perry farm in Bournedale—was a fitting place to begin this maritime project. After Belmont shoveled, he said, "I promise in digging the first shovelful not to desert the task until the last shovelful has been dug." He also promised the canal would be finished in three and one-half years. After the ceremony, according to Mrs. Belmont, some of the earth moved by her husband's tiny shovel was taken back to New York City in an empty bean can found on the Perry farm.

Decades of talk and no action had produced legions of skeptics, and many Cape Codders remained doubtful about this latest try. Belmont was aware of this. "It is a poor and stupid argument that the past failures to build this canal should still nurse skeptics on the subject," he told reporters. Four days later a story on the ceremony in the *Yarmouth Register* referred to a "noticeable lack of enthusiasm among the spectators when the official spoonful of sod was chiseled from Mother Earth and fell with a dull thud on the turf."

For some time a few schooners and lighters and a tugboat off Scusset Beach remained the only signs of construction. The summer was half over before the first dredge arrived. On August 2 an old ladder dredge, the *Kennedy*, was towed up Buzzards Bay and started to dig the approach channel. The persistent clanking of her endless chain of buckets would become infamous to permanent and summer residents alike. Although of an obsolete design, the *Kennedy* was capable of steady work twenty-four hours per day, every day. A few weeks later a second dredge appeared. She was No. 1 of the Coastwise Dredging Company, with a five-cubic-yard clam shell for digging. She moved ahead of the *Kennedy*, working down to twelve feet deep between Mashnee Island and Monument Beach. Both machines loaded the spoil from the bottom onto scows, which dumped it at sea. The plan was to cut a channel through to the Monument River so hydraulic dredges could dig the isthmus. Larger dredges were to be brought in later to complete the approach channel.

The incessant banging and clanking of the dredges wore heavily on the nerves of local residents. One anonymous wag was to pen a verse titled *Buzzards Bay Dredging Dirge*:

Rich Residents Say
  Cape Dredgers Gay
    Drive Sleep Away
      From Buzzards Bay
Oh, Please go 'way and let us sleep,
You dredgers there make din so deep
That day or night we lose our rest,
Our bliss you blight—You're sure a pest—
So please go 'way and let us sleep.

Fortunately for Sandwich residents, dredging was slower in getting under way on the eastern end of the canal. Furst-Clark finally brought its largest hydraulic—or suction—dredge to the cape on October 16. A cut through the beach at Sandwich was necessary for two reasons. First, the fleet working the breakwater, out in the open, had no nearby shelter. Plymouth was the nearest harbor, but that was sixteen miles away; Provincetown was twenty-one miles distant. It was already mid-October, when mean nor'easters frequently move in on the cape. Thus, with an opening through the beach into the old Lockwood ditch a port for the stone fleet would be at hand. Second, the cut would also make it possible to dredge right through the winter in a protected area.

As it turned out, however, the *General MacKenzie*, a large suction dredge, arrived too late. With two weeks of pleasant weather, she could have opened a channel into the Lockwood ditch. Instead, during the next fifty-three days the weather was so bad she was towed to Provincetown Harbor and back a dozen times, while the stone fleet spent most of its time running for cover at Plymouth. The *General MacKenzie* could only work a total of eight days. A seagoing tugboat, the *Buccaneer*, had to stand by to move her at the cost of $150 per day.

On November 29 a sudden gale moved in from the northeast, sending the stone fleet for cover at Plymouth and two lighters crashing onto the beach, where the crews were rescued. The *General MacKenzie*, though nearly lost, reached Provincetown at the end of a tow rope. Furst-Clark decided to wait for spring. When the weather calmed, the company towed the *General MacKenzie* to Plymouth to spend the winter in the comparative tranquility of its inner harbor. The two dredges on the western end of the canal were also withdrawn.

The prime effort had been to build the breakwater at Sandwich, but only 46,000 tons of granite had been dropped since the third week of June. The amount of granite visible was slight—from the beach out into the water about seventy-five feet. The rest was on the bottom of the bay. Complicating matters was the way the subcontractor, the Gilbert Transportation Company, supplied the granite. Since the engineers were in a hurry to start, they had accepted shipment of the granite aboard lumber schooners, which were poorly suited for carrying stone. Naturally, this slowed things down. But an even worse problem was that of short weight. It started early, according to Durham:

> The first bit of rock was part of a load of one-hundred twenty-five tons. . . . The contractor claimed one-hundred fifty tons and, as my estimate was based on bow and stern readings in fairly rough water, I let it stand. . . . What seemed curious was that the subsequent errors were all in the subcontractor's favor. . . . The difference between his bills of lading and our measurements of his rock loads increased until all his captains knew we were suspicious and one old Maine sailor when asked by our inspector how much he had in his latest load said, "Wa'al, the bill of lading calls for one-thousand tons. If I had it aboard I'd sink."

Faced with widespread evidence of false weights, a grim Michael Degnon fired the stone contractor, Samuel R. Rosov, and decided he would build the breakwater himself when the weather eased. To make way for a sure start on the eastern end of the canal in the spring, Furst-Clark brought two steam excavators by rail from Chicago to ground near the Lockwood ditch, where they were assembled in December of 1909 and early January of the next year.

Since the *General MacKenzie* was too valuable to risk outside the beach, another approach, better suited to winter, was agreed upon. If a small dredge could be found, and the right tides, she could float over the bar at the mouth of the Scusset River and through the marshes to Lockwood's ditch, digging eastward from there to open up an entrance through the beach. Then the *General MacKenzie* could come inside this channel to work. It was an idea someone should have thought of the previous summer when the vice president of the Construction Company, Comdr. Jacob W. Miller, was urging Belmont to get the contractors to put more plant to work. If they had, the

General MacKenzie could have been dredging west during the winter instead of lying idle at Plymouth.

A small dredge, the *Nahant*, was rented from the Eastern Dredging Company, and after a wait for the right tide—it had to be higher than usual —she slid across the bar. The steam excavators dug a channel through shoals between Tuppers Creek and the Lockwood cut, and the *Nahant* came through.

With the passage for the *Nahant* completed through the marshes, the two land excavators were moved west "to scoop off the over-burden in the dry," according to Parsons. At the time, it seemed like a good idea. It was not, not with that equipment. The land excavators, or drag-lines, were large, ungainly contraptions, weighing 110 tons each. Their 100-foot booms swung eight-ton buckets out, dropped them, then hauled them back toward the machine. Because of the area's rough ground and swamps, the excavators had to be horsed around on hickory rollers. It was not easy. Whoever designed them—and his name is lost to us—forgot about the need for mobility. Whoever bought them—in this case, the Furst-Clark Company—should have studied the ground they were to be used on first. In the swampy areas, they sank; in solid but rough areas, they were nearly impossible to move. Nonetheless, the indefatigable John W. Dalton, Sandwich reporter for the *Boston Globe* and an ever-optimistic supporter of the canal, wrote in praise of the excavators: "they handle seven- to eight-hundred cubic yards a day, working night and day like the dredges." One excavator was kept on until November of 1910, the other until the following February, working without distinction. Parsons finally dismissed them with the comment: "they are most unsatisfactory . . . not adapted to the soil."

The *Nahant* started to work on January 24, 1910, digging toward Cape Cod Bay to make way for the *General MacKenzie*. Fifteen-hundred feet of sand had filled in the entrance to the Lockwood effort from the beach. The *Nahant* had a small, one-cubic-yard orange peel bucket, a steel ball with fingers that separated like the segmented fruit, then clamped shut on the material to be dredged; that was suspended from an extralong boom to drop sand on shore to either side. It was the first digging the isthmus had seen since Frederick Lockwood's machine had stopped more than eighteen years before. The machine dug through the isthmus night and day, as had the two dredges in Buzzards Bay.

In two and one-half months the *Nahant* reached the sea. To the north, the crew of the *General MacKenzie* had been getting her ready after several months of inactivity. A tugboat brought her down from Plymouth on April 8, 1910, and moved her through the cut in the beach. She was positioned with her pipe down and her discharge line out the stern, pumping sand into the marshes to the north. The job went well at first, as only sand and a little light clay were encountered. Although the big cutter blade occasionally clogged on stumps and rocks, and once broke down on the backbone of a whale, the going generally was easy. This encouraged Furst-Clark to dig in tandem with a second hydraulic dredge. This machine, *No. 9* of the Southern Dredging Company, moved ahead of the *General MacKenzie*, digging down to seventeen feet; the *General MacKenzie* followed, removing an additional six feet.

Construction on the breakwater was going nicely. Degnon was buying stone from the Rockport Granite Company at Pigeon Cove, Cape Ann, an excellent source about thirty-five miles north of Boston. The inadequate lumber schooners were gone, replaced by sloops designed to carry stone and by scows, the easiest vessels to unload quickly. There were no questions about the weight of the stone now.

On the western end of the canal, the two dredges in the Buzzards Bay approach channel had been excavating since March of 1910. Early in June the same year another kind of dredge joined the fleet. The *Bothfeld* was a dipper; it operated like a floating steam shovel, digging the bottom and dropping the material into scows. A small hydraulic dredge with a twelve-inch discharge pipe was brought in under the railroad trestle and put to work in the Monument River. Two more dredges joined the growing fleet at the western end of the canal during the summer. The *Neponset*, a small clam shell like the *Nahant* (which had been withdrawn), worked in the upper end of Buzzards Bay, and the *Onondaga*, a nine-yard dipper, was farther out in the approach channel. By Labor Day there were six machines in the western division, and the two hydraulics on the east were approaching the town line dividing Sandwich and Bourne by fall.

The Canal Company had agreed under its charter to provide bridges and other crossings to the canal, including a ferry at Bournedale. The substructure for the railroad bridge at Buzzards Bay was started in November of 1909. On May 10, 1910, steel workers of Merritt, Chapman Derrick and Wrecking Company were riveting steel for the deck and superstructure. By September 20 the bridge was finished, although a delay in track relocation prevented the use of the bridge until early November of 1911.

In August of 1910 the piers were started for the Bourne highway bridge three-quarters of a mile east of the rail bridge. The firm of Holbrook, Cabot and Rollins, which earlier had bid on parts of the canal work, was the subcontractor. The Bourne Bridge, an electrically operated drawbridge with two eighty-foot cantilever spans, which replaced an older structure, was finished across the Monument River at a point the dredges had not reached. The bridge itself was ready in May of 1911, and the approach roads were completed in October. The Bourne Bridge was the first of two bridges for motor vehicles to span the canal, and it also had a single track for trolleys of the New Bedford and Onset Street Railway Company, which ran as far as Monument Beach.

The third bridge to go into service across the canal was a temporary wooden structure that was mostly a trestle with a small draw span, erected in 1911 at Sagamore adjacent to the Keith Car and Manufacturing works. Steel work on the Sagamore Bridge began in the spring of 1912, with completion the following winter. Then the wooden span was dismantled and moved to Bournedale, opposite the railroad station, where the Canal Company had agreed to run a free ferry across the canal.

All three bridges were designed to provide a channel opening of 160 feet. The water passage was twenty feet narrower, or 140 feet, because of wooden fenders built in front and partially to the sides of the bridge piers to protect them from collisions with ships. Main bridge piers were sunk sufficiently deep to allow an eventual channel depth of thirty feet if an expansion was ever deemed necessary.

Most canal schemes had stressed the commercial advantages to the towns along the route. Belmont and the others in the present venture had also played up this opportunity to gain popular support, promising an open port for Sandwich along the canal by January 1, 1911. Degnon's stone crews had been busy during 1910, laying enough granite out from the beach for the breakwater to offer some protection from storms out of the north and east. Fishing boats had started to use the canal for refuge from storms in the fall of that year, and on December 14 the first cargo arrived in Sandwich on a commercial vessel. The Canal Company had been true to its word. The coal barge, of whaleback design, entered the canal with a familiar visitor, the tugboat *Mary Arnold*, handling the tow. The *Yarmouth Register* had made many an acid comment in the past about one canal idea or another, but now all was forgiven. Its generally favorable story on the event began, " 'Three cheers and a tiger for August Belmont, Capt. Miller and the other officers of the Cape Cod Canal Co.,' said an old sailorman on Monday, as he stood on the beach at Sandwich and sighted the barge *Cassie*, with 2,000 tons of coal aboard, her full capacity, being towed into the partially completed waterway into the new port of this old and historic town." The editor was a convert.

The year 1910 had not been a bad one for dredging on the western end of the canal. Although the approach channel was not finished, it was excavated down to fifteen feet in the center all the way to the railroad bridge at Buzzards Bay. About one-third of the work had been done there. By

Christmas the engineers were reporting to the Joint Board that about 25 percent of the total project was completed. It is difficult to see how they derived this figure, but one thing is certain—it was too high.

There were signs of serious trouble on the eastern end of the canal. The *General MacKenzie* had been running into stiff clay, cobbles, cemented gravel, and boulders too large to handle. Dipper dredges became necessary after the eastern end had been dug for about one and one-half miles. *No. 9* had been withdrawn, and Furst-Clark purchased three old dipper dredges— the *National*, the *Capitol*, and the *International*—and a small hydraulic, the *Federal*. The three dippers reached Buzzards Bay in November and December of 1910, and the *National* and the *Capitol* were towed at once around the cape to handle the heavy material that was clogging and disabling the *General MacKenzie*. They worked through the winter, making little progress through Sagamore Hill. Five dredges had to be withdrawn from Buzzards Bay for the winter. One that remained inadvertently destroyed a wild oyster bed that brought on the company a large law suit.

With the return of good weather in the spring of 1911, two hydraulics entered the Monument River while the dippers worked the approach channel between the head of Buzzards Bay and Monument Beach. After the dippers hit mammoth boulders they were incapable of handling, divers had to be brought in to shatter them with dynamite. Engineers first plotted a boulder's size from the surface with a sounding lead. Then the divers, working from small wooden scows holding air compressors on the deck operated by two assistants turning wheels, set their charges. This was a slow and cautious process in murky waters, whose chilling temperatures limited the time divers could spend below. After the charges were placed, boats and divers had to move back from the blasting area. Engineers on the dredges fumed because their company was paid by the cubic yard for removing material. But even while no work was being done both the dredges and the tugboats coantinued paying two full crews and burning coal to keep up steam. Some of the boulders weighed more than one hundred tons, requiring several charges of 25 to 200 pounds each. At times divers would attach slings to boulders, which would then be hoisted out of the channel by lighters or, occasionally, by dredges.

The dredges started hitting boulders in Buzzards Bay at twenty feet. At Sagamore Hill, they were found at eighteen feet. In some places there were nests of them—huge chunks of glacial debris that Parsons had earlier dismissed as "no problem."

On April 1, 1911, the *General MacKenzie* returned to work, moving to the heading in front of the *Capitol* and the *National*. This arrangement was more effective than the two dippers working by themselves with their five- and six-yard buckets.

If the material encountered by the dredges had been sand or mud, much more would have been accomplished by this time. All of Furst-Clark's experience had been with soft material that could be quickly removed by big suction dredges like the *General MacKenzie*. Now the firm found itself up against material that was anything but soft, and the dredges, especially on the eastern end of the channel, were falling behind schedule. It was a costly lesson, learned late. Something had to be done or the canal would be completed years after it should have been and at far greater expense than anticipated.

Parsons originally had suggested using steam shovels to dig "in the dry" in the middle of the isthmus. His suggestion, made before work began in 1909, had not been followed. Now it was decided to test it, warily, on a limited basis. In May of 1911 the C. W. Reynolds Company started excavating "in the dry" near Sagamore—but with laborers using shovels. That was not what Parsons had in mind. The arrival of a steam shovel on narrow-gauge tracks in August replaced the inefficient manual effort. Work also started at another location, near Bournedale at Station No. 255. (Points every 100 feet, starting at the end of the breakwater, were designated "stations," with numbers increasing westward.) There the Wilson and English Company put in two steam shovels and a small network of construction tracks with dump cars to carry material off to the sides of the cut. Although the tracks had to be moved frequently as the digging progressed, it was a generally good operation.

Near the end of the summer the fleet in Buzzards Bay numbered about twenty-five vessels, including ten dredges. Tugboats were busy shuttling empty scows to the dredges and taking loaded ones to sea for dumping. Of course, it was a twenty-four-hour per day operation, every day. More than four hundred men were employed—easily the largest construction job ever undertaken on the cape. With dredges at both headings and three steam shovels in the middle, an average of about one-quarter-million cubic yards of earth per month was being moved; if the canal was to open in June of 1913, however, that average would have to be doubled. Bigger equipment was necessary. To get it, Furst-Clark went to the American Locomotive Company at Paterson, New Jersey, and contracted for two large dipper dredges to be built along the canal, one at Buzzards Bay, the other at Sagamore. As designed, they were the largest of their kind. Ways were built at the two locations while the steel was prefabricated at Paterson; launching was anticipated by late winter of 1912.

Elsewhere, there were these developments by the end of 1911:

The breakwater was about three-quarters finished. Degnon's stone fleet had been dropping Cape Ann granite on the 3,000-foot breakwater from March until December and 286,000 tons were in place.

Railroad track crews had relocated most of the single-track line that had crossed and recrossed the valley to its new route along the south bank of the canal. Trains for "down Cape" and Woods Hole were using the new bascule bridge—with a single lift arm—at the south end of the rebuilt railroad yards at Buzzards Bay. All that was left of the old "down Cape" track north of the Monument River was a spur to a lumber yard just west of the new Bourne Bridge.

Charles Thompson had been busy persuading landowners to sell, and most of the additional land needed for the canal was in hand.

The western approach channel up Buzzards Bay had been dredged to fifteen feet from Wings Neck Light to the railroad bridge, a distance of five miles. Dredges were in the Monument River, while the canal on the eastern end was more than two miles in from the end of the breakwater.

Despite the large number of boulders and the dearth of work on the middle section of the isthmus, there was no slackening of optimism in the public statements of Canal Company officials, especially from the vice president, Commodore Miller. He had come to the organization from J. P. Morgan's New England Steamship Company after service in the United States Navy, where he had attained the rank he still used before his name. Miller was a tall, handsome man with a ready smile, which he turned on frequently in public or when photographers were around. In the argot of the day there was no such term as "PR," but Miller functioned as a public relations man on the company's behalf. He, too, had been in Panama on isthmian surveys—a point he often made in conversation or speeches, for that mammoth undertaking by the United States government was within a few years of seeing its first ship transit the jungles.

During a speech in Richmond, Virginia, in October of 1911, before the Atlantic Deeper Waterways Association, Miller—though he knew the facts to be otherwise—stated that, "there is already built a breakwater containing over 400,000 tons of granite as a protection against any northeast gales." The Gilbert Transportation Company apparently was not the only source of inflated weights of delivered stone. Of course, Miller's reference to a breakwater "already built" was equally untrue. In reality, at the then-present rate of construction the canal could not open until 1915, or not much earlier at any rate. But Miller never let such facts get in the way of delivering an uplifting address. In December, before an appreciative audience from the New England Society in New York City, he told the businessmen, many of whom had interests in shipping by water, that "the bare-bended arm of Masssachusetts is about to lose its threatening terrors, and in a year the Cape will become an island."

At Richmond, Miller had referred to the purchase of land "along the banks for the purpose of establishing manufactures already demanding factory sites." This had been a standard theme in company literature and speeches by its executives for several years, but it just was not happening.

Belmont, too, watered the truth. For example, on December 7 he addressed the National Rivers and Harbors Congress in Washington, D.C. Before such a group the problems at the cape seemed to vanish. "The work is practically half finished," he proclaimed. He paused for a round of applause, which came, then reported that the project was "on the road to rapid and positive completion." He also got in a dig at the skeptics, since they were safely at a distance. "During our life as a company, working at this undertaking at the Cape, phantom after phantom, conjured by long years of waiting and failure, colored by the croakings of retired seafarers and other loquacious wiseacres, have vanished." Referring to the future, Belmont made a brief but prophetic comment about "the possible use, in time of war, the Cape Cod Canal might be obliged to serve." There were those who said it was an early move toward asking for government help. Belmont denied it, saying, "we have asked for no help, and want none."

Back on the cape, the steam shovels and some dredges worked through the winter of 1912, but the hopes of the Canal Company were on those two big machines being built along the canal banks. Both were of the same design. Powered by thirteen separate steam engines, each would have a ten-cubic-yard dipper for soft material with an eight-yard box for boulders. The *Governor Herrick* was built at Sagamore, just outside the fence at Keith Car and Manufacturing Company and a few feet from the canal. Her hull was to be launched on Palm Sunday, March 31, 1912, at 10 A.M. When one of the ways sank a little, she slid as far as the bank and stuck there. Some of those on hand tried pushing. They failed. A tugboat in the canal did some pulling. She failed also. It was an embarrassing time. A group of canal officials and their wives were dressed up for the occasion, which included christening the hull with wine. Journalists from as far away as New Bedford and Boston were on hand. So was a large crowd. Everyone stood around, waiting. Some thought it was funny—and quite typical of how the whole canal project had gone. Apparently Belmont's "phantoms" had not quite been exorcised. About one week later the hull finally made it to the water, where her machinery and superstructure were added. In July, behind schedule like everything else, the *Governor Herrick* moved west toward the channel to dig. Her sister dredge, the *Governor Warfield*, was completed in August. Both were rated at 100,000 cubic yards per month; they averaged a little under that as they worked toward each other from opposite headings.

The need to get more of the canal under construction led the Construction Company to consider building a huge marine railway on which the *General MacKenzie* could be moved overland to a lake created by a dam on the Monument River. But the problems of such a venture were too great, and the idea was dropped. Instead, the company dismantled one of the hydraulic dredges, the *Federal*, and installed her equipment on a hull built inland near Bournedale. She started digging west in August, enlarging her own lake as she went.

Parsons also decided to step up the steam shovel work, diverting the Monument River to the east so that the E. W. Foley Company of New York City would have a dry area in which to work. Foley brought in more shovels, using narrow-gauge equipment with two-and-one-half-cubic-yard dippers and four-yard wooden dump cars. The small construction trains were pushed out of the trench by saddletank steam engines on tracks that were moved frequently. The deeper the shovels dug the more boulders they struck, but the rocks were not the problem they had been for the dredges. The shovels pushed them aside for the powder men, who shattered them for riprap.

Electric pumps with steam pumps on standby removed groundwater from the trench, since the shovels penetrated ten feet below sea level, which was twenty feet below groundwater. The pumps easily handled it; water was never a problem in the "dry" digging areas. The shovels were a success, eventually removing over eight hundred thousand cubic yards of material from 6,800 feet of the isthmus from Station No. 208 west to Station No. 276.

In the spring of 1913 Parsons invited Belmont to see the progress. In June, Belmont, his wife, and a few investors toured the job by tugboat, winding up the inspection tour in the steam shovel section on a flat car with benches—a far cry from the Mineola.

Later that year Degnon finished the breakwater. Now the only major work remaining was the rest of the excavation. While the steam shovels cleaned out the trench, the *Governor Herrick* and the *Governor Warfield* were excavating at either end of the channel with other dredges behind them. Four natural dams left in the steam shovel section divided it into three areas. One, beginning at Station No. 208, was 800 feet long; the next, from Station No. 216 to No. 234, was 1,800 feet long, and the longest, 4,200 feet, extended from Station No. 234 to No. 276. As the dredges worked toward each other and broke through each dam, canal water flooded that section. The dredge then deepened the channel at that point to roughly eighteen feet at low water.

By the spring of 1914, there was one dam left between the two sections of the canal—at Station No. 234, slightly west of the midpoint of the isthmus. The dam was a pile of sand, at least on top, running across the waterway at a slight angle to the southeast. As the last barrier to a tidal waterway, it even got a name: Foley's Dyke. It was to this spot that August Perry Belmont invited company directors and investors to make an inspection trip on April 21, 1914, and to witness a ceremonial "blending of the waters." For the occasion a narrow wooden sluiceway had been built across the top of the dyke which, when open, would channel tidal water back and forth. Belmont had two bottles with glass stoppers, each containing water from one end of the canal. He removed the stoppers, then poured water from both so it mixed while falling to the ground. "May the meeting of these waters bring happiness and prosperity to our country and save some of the misery which the waters of the Cape have caused in the past," he intoned. A little shoveling on the west side of the dam and the water in the channel trickled through. Belmont swung one of the shovels briefly, then reached across the small flow of water and shook hands with Parsons. In a front page story several days later, the *Bourne Independent* estimated the crowd that day as about one hundred—a generous figure. A subhead declared: "Cape Cod Now an Island."

It was all dredging now; the steam shovels were gone. The *Governor Herrick* and the *Governor Warfield* were within sight of each other as spring turned to summer. Although the contractors wanted more time to dig a fifteen-foot channel right up to both sides of Foley's Dyke, Belmont decided to cut the last barrier on the Fourth of July, simultaneously marking the 275th Anniversary of Sandwich. Workers with shovels took a wedge out of the top of the dam and the high tide from Cape Cod Bay did the rest. The water poured through, chewing a huge gash through most of the dyke and churning trees, boulders, and sand. It was a wild, frightening scene, the water moving like a millrace at flood time. Later, when the tide dropped and the water calmed, Belmont and his son rowed the chief engineer and Mrs. Parsons through the gap where Foley's Dyke had been.

With the official opening of the canal set for July 29, the two big dredges had to deepen about one thousand feet of the remaining shallows. The tidal current at some stages fairly boiled over the dredges as it squeezed through the narrow channel. The long, steel spuds of the two machines were driven as far into the bottom as possible, acting as anchors to hold them in place. So fierce was the westward current that the stern spuds on the *Gover-*

nor Herrick broke. To hold her firmly in position, the dredge *International* was brought up stern first and lashed tightly to the *Herrick's* stern. Then the *International's* spuds were driven down to replace the broken ones of the *Herrick*. The two worked right up to July 28, when they were withdrawn to permit passage of the opening day's fleet.

Although the canal had at least fifteen feet at low water, a little more in some places, it still was not finished to its charter depth. So why did Belmont open it? A combination of factors probably helped make up his mind. Money may have been the most important: all the cash flow had been out, but the speedy collection of tolls would reverse that. Furthermore, the Kiel Canal in Germany had opened in June of 1914, and the Panama Canal was to open about the middle of August. With canals so much in the news, Belmont's waterway was bound to reap a publicity harvest. Or so it seemed. Then there was the annual summer cruise of the New York Yacht Club—Belmont was one of its better known members—which wished to use the canal during that mass voyage Down East in August. Could fellow members have applied a little pressure?

Toward the end of July, extensive mobilization for war in Europe dominated the newspapers, pushing the opening of the Cape Cod Canal to inside pages, except in New England. Still, advertisements were placed on the maritime pages of newspapers in large cities where potential canal traffic might originate. Two such notices appeared in the *Boston Globe*. The first, on Thursday, July 23, read: "Open for daylight traffic, July 30 at eight A.M. for vessels not exceeding 15 ft. draft." On the following Monday, July 27 the second notice read: "fog 50 per cent less than present route . . . no locks . . . 70 miles saved . . . open to tows of same draft on Sept. 1 . . . open day and night on August 15th, 1914."

The stage was set. Now for the big moment, the opening itself. Belmont read a lot of history, borrowing from it when it suited his purposes. He seized on the glorious opening of the Suez Canal, hoping that a similar start would lead to the same extraordinary success for his endeavor. Invitations to participate in the opening ceremony were mailed early in July to the United States Navy and to friends, politicians, bankers, industrialists, railroad and maritime executives, and canal investors who had large yachts. The navy and many of the most influential members of the establishment accepted. Belmont's canal would open grandly, with a parade of ships.

3

August Perry Belmont's Private Ditch

JULY 29, 1914. The sun rose bright and warm over Cape Cod Bay, shimmering on the waves that lapped against Michael Degnon's new breakwater. The preceding week had been rainy, but now the skies were clear, with the promise of success for Belmont's at-long-last completed venture. Ships had gathered in New Bedford Harbor; by late morning the parade was ready to begin.

The procession sailed to the blasts of steam whistles from nearby factories and other ships. At its head, gleaming white, was the two-year-old *Rose Standish*, an excursion steamer Belmont had rented from the Nantasket Beach Steamboat Company of Boston. The vessel, 215 feet long and almost sixty feet wide across her paddlewheels, actually became the first passenger ship to travel the canal the day before, when she steamed west to join the fleet in New Bedford. After making the transit in a little under one hour, the general manager of the line, who was aboard, pronounced the canal to be "in fine shape." Now, for the formal opening, the steamer was packed with Belmont's guests, many of whom had come by chartered trains from New York, Boston, and Newport.

Behind the *Rose Standish* was the destroyer *McDougall*, carrying Franklin D. Roosevelt, the assistant secretary of the navy. Then came the yachts, seven of them, led by Belmont's eighty-one-foot *Scout*. Six other destroyers served as escorts to the approach channel entrance off Wings Neck, where two revenue cutters and two navy submarines were standing by. The *Rose Standish* led the way up the Buzzards Bay entrance of the canal through Phinneys Harbor Channel. Yachts seemed to be everywhere along the route, tearing back and forth, whistling at the vessels in the official line. Just before the second turn in the channel to the west of Gray Gables Point, some of the dredges, tugboats, scows, and lighters of the work fleet were either anchored or tied to pile clusters, known as dolphins. The work fleet had steam up and added its whistle blasts to the noise. All the ships, even the scows, had flags and streamers flying.

The *Rose Standish* came around Gray Gables Point and headed straight for the opening at the rail bridge, past a couple of lighters on the starboard side of the channel. More whistles. At 1:31 P.M., the bow of the steamer knifed through the red, white, and blue bunting stretched across the canal between two dolphins. Great crowds were on both sides of the waterway now, cheering, waving. The vessels in the fleet whistled in reply. Following the *Rose Standish* came the destroyer *McDougall* with sailors all in white, waving to those ashore. The *Scout* was next, followed by the seven palatial yachts. Last was the tugboat *Orion* from Boston, carrying the reporters. John W. Dalton, the *Boston Globe's* Sandwich reporter and ever-faithful courier of canal propaganda, was in charge. It was a position he relished and had certainly earned, since no journalist had been as tireless in promoting the Boston, Cape Cod and New York Canal Company as Dalton.

Not only were businesses near the canal decorated, but many homes displayed flags. The Keith Car and Manufacturing Company and a golf club in Sagamore were decked with flags and bunting. The owners of many cars who had driven to the canal waited until the fleet passed by, then followed down the winding roads toward Sandwich.

At the eastern entrance of the canal the *Scout* moved along side the *Rose Standish* to pick up Belmont, Massachusetts Gov. David I. Walsh, and several others and take them ashore for the celebration at Sandwich. The fleet continued out into Cape Cod Bay, where the last ship signaled with her whistle; all vessels then turned and went back through the canal in reverse order.

A parade of fifty floats and about five thousand spectators had moved from the center of Sandwich to Town Neck and were there when Belmont and the governor arrived to the strains of "Hail to the Chief." The speeches were short, as the official canal opening was to be held in Bourne a little later. The chairman of the reception committee, William L. Nye, presented Belmont with a large silver loving cup on behalf of the town's citizens. Belmont traced his Sandwich connections during a short speech. Recalling that a daughter of one of the town's founders, Edmund Freeman, had married Edward Perry, he said that "from this episode arose that little event on Lake Erie in 1812 [*sic*], the opening of the ports of Japan to commerce in 1854 . . . for which the Perrys have, I believe, earned honorable mention." Governor Walsh described Belmont's courage "as greater than the nation or the state."

Meanwhile, the Parade of Ships was moving west toward Buzzards Bay. The ships had come east with the current, which had changed when they were in the canal westbound. Captains preferred sailing with the current in narrow waters because it made vessels easier to control. Current through the canal was stronger than the engineers had predicted, although its intensity varied with the time of the tide. It had reached five knots when the yachts reached the rail bridge near where they were to tie up at assigned dolphins. The yachts made it with some difficulty, and the last ship, the *Rose Standish* —with paddlewheels thrashing in reverse—was swept right by a small dock on Bourne Neck and carried out some distance into Buzzards Bay. Her captain managed to get her turned around within a few minutes. After she was tied up, the guests poured off and walked a short distance to a large tent for the opening day program.

The main speaker, former New York City Mayor Seth Low, made the point that New York people built the canal, because they "take kindly to canal construction partly by inherited instinct and partly as the result of experience." He said he thought he knew why the Commonwealth of Massachusetts had never built the canal: "The genius of New England for a century has expressed itself . . . in manufacture, and the significance of the canal to manufacture is indirect, not direct." Low said that Belmont's New York City subway experience induced the banker to build the canal, and that, like the subway, the canal "was the offer of better facilities for traffic that already existed."

In contrast to what had just been said, Belmont himself thought New England had a great deal to do with the building of the Cape Cod Canal, since his maternal ancestors were Cape Codders. Before dedicating the new waterway to the "commerce of the United States," he said, "We have been building the greatest life-saving institution on the Atlantic, and through our efforts the historic graveyard of the coast may be closed. Personally, should it serve no other purpose than the saving of thousands of lives from perishing off the Cape, I shall feel my own efforts are repaid."

All round, it had been a good day for August Perry Belmont and his new canal. He had been cheered and praised. The photographs taken that July afternoon reveal a relaxed, sixty-one-year-old man with a most satisfied smile.

At 8:00 A.M. the next day the canal opened for business with a small yacht paying the first transit toll: eight dollars. The day's gross was fifty-one dollars. Thirteen days later a railroad tugboat and three empty schooner-barges, returning from a coal trip, went west with a small harbor tugboat to steady the stern barge. This tow was the first commercial business. A few days after that the lighting system went into service, with poles opposite each other every 500 feet to allow round-the-clock operation. The canal's narrow channel permitted only one-way traffic, which was controlled by lights at each end.

The charter allowed the Canal Company to charge whatever it wished for tolls, and at first they were high. Steamers, both passenger and freight, and yachts paid the most: ten cents per gross ton. The barge operators got a better break with a seven-cent charge on each ton of cargo and five cents per ton on gross weight when transiting light or in ballast. Most of that early traffic consisted of yachts, but the company expected to attract many more tugboats and barges when channel depth reached twenty-five feet. Most tugboats in coastal service drew no more than ten feet (a few drew twelve), but their tows, big schooner-barges close to 200 feet long, drew more than twelve feet when loaded. Consequently, most of them, when north or south bound, continued using Pollock Rip Channel, while a few saved time via the canal only when southbound and traveling light.

The company provided a tugboat service through the canal for vessels requiring it; usually two tugboats were berthed next to the rail bridge, and one at Sandwich. Towing fees, based on vessel size and weight, were another source of income, as were anchorage fees.

For captains unfamiliar with the canal, a private organization, the Cape Cod Canal Pilot's Association, provided a pilot to take vessels through. Each pilot had to have a mariner's license and a canal endorsement. Skippers taking their own vessels through had to have an indorsement on their tickets from the Steamboat Inspection Service. Ships could either telephone ahead, giving their estimated time of arrival and requesting a pilot, or raise signal flags before they reached Wings Neck Light or Sandwich Control Station. The pilot collected his fee before he left the vessel.

A few months after the opening, Furst-Clark gave up trying to finish dredging the canal—moving scows for traffic caused too many delays. The *Governor Warfield* and some other equipment were turned over to the Construction Company. Not only did Furst-Clark lose money, as reportedly did all the subcontractors, but Michael Degnon left the canal to file for bankruptcy before the waterway opened. Besides the dredges operated by the Construction Company, two groups of divers continued to locate boulders for destruction by blasting or removal by lighters with slings. The first of two large hydraulic machines started to deepen the channel in October of 1914.

In November, a foreign freighter went west through the canal giving rise to hopes that larger, better paying customers would start using the waterway. The 350-foot vessel *Tenbergen*, the largest ship to make a transit through the canal that first year, was in ballast and had no difficulty in the shoal channel. Her skipper wrote the Canal Company, praising the ease of passage and the helpfulness of canal employees; the company reprinted parts of the letter in promotional literature. But it did not help recruit business, which for 1914 amounted to $33,000 in tolls, paid by the owners of 582 vessels. Since maintenance and operating costs during this period were $80,000, the company realized a net loss for the first five months of $47,000. The second year, the first full one, up to July 30, 1916, saw income rise to $122,665, while operating and maintenance costs rose to $199,139—a loss of $76,474. Of course, dredging costs had been high until the entire channel was dredged to a depth of twenty-five feet in April of 1916.

Traffic steadily increased with the greater depth of the canal. In 1915, with the channel twenty feet deep, 2,689 vessels made transits; the following year the number of vessels reached 4,634, with a gross tonnage of 3.5 million. The passenger count in 1916 alone climbed from almost 70,000 to 140,000, primarily because the Eastern Steamship Lines made a seasonal contract to send its New York-Boston steamers through on every passage. The Canal Company gave the line a special rate far below its advertised tolls, and twice a day from April to October its big white ships cruised through.

Still, business was far below expectations, and many mariners would not use the canal. The current, which could reach six knots in that narrow channel, frightened many skippers, as did the fear of colliding with a bridge. A ground fog condition, called vapor, usually occurring around Bournedale, often cut visibility to the point of stopping all traffic. It was prevalent after midnight and lasted past dawn. Two accidents within five months of each other in 1916 worsened the bad reputation the canal had among maritime people. Both involved whaleback freighters. First, the *William Chisolm* ran into the bank at Bournedale while moving east with coal on July 16. The mishap forced New York-Boston passenger steamers to go back to Pollock Rip Channel as there was not enough room to pass the *Chisolm*, although smaller ships continued to use the waterway. In two weeks, salvage vessels moved her and traffic returned to normal patterns.

Then, on December 13, the S.S. *Bayport* veered out of the channel and struck the bank. Quickly the Canal Company ordered salvage operations. The following day tugboats pulled the *Bayport* off and into mid-channel where she sank, completely blocking the waterway. Efforts to raise her failed. The canal was closed for three months until finally the *Bayport* was demolished with explosives. There was no income during that time, which was bad enough, but the accident scared off some mariners who had not already been discouraged by the canal's narrow channel and strong current. Some editorialists claimed the *Bayport* accident finished the canal.

In an effort to attract more business, the Canal Company reduced its tolls. Steamers and yachts now paid eight cents per gross ton; barges, five cents per cargo ton loaded and three cents per gross ton empty. In 1917, traffic was off by over one thousand vessels, and the company reported a $48,000 loss. Because tugboat service accounted for a considerable part of the loss, the company reduced its fleet to two boats; early the following year the tugboat service was eliminated. The big passenger steamers of Eastern

Steamship Lines—the *Massachusetts, Bunker Hill*, and *Old Colony*—returned for their second season in the spring, but with no reduction in tolls. Meanwhile, the United States had gone off to war in April, but this had no effect on traffic, which continued the downhill slide brought on by the sinking of the *Bayport*.

Coastal tows carrying coal, the industrial life blood of New England, were supposed to be the biggest source of canal revenue. This business was dominated by railroads, which operated large marine fleets (very little coal entered New England by rail). The Reading Railroad, a major owner of Pennsylvania anthracite mines, brought its coal to Port Reading, New Jersey, opposite Staten Island, and to Philadelphia. Reading had the largest coal fleet on the coast, comprising fifteen tugboats and more than sixty schooner-barges. As the biggest single source of coal for New England, the Reading Railroad should have been a leading canal customer, but its tows inexplicably continued to use Nantucket Sound and Pollock Rip Channel. On the other hand, Erie Railroad tows used the canal exclusively, since the line's president, F. D. Underwood, was a director of the Canal Company. And the Pennsylvania and Lehigh Valley railroads also were frequent customers.

Huge amounts of coal—more than 10 million tons per year—entered northern New England by water to be used in manufacturing, making city gas, and heating homes. Railroads had coal docks at many northern New England ports from which they moved the black stuff in hopper cars to their customers. The principal ship of transport for coal was the molded or schooner-barge, a two- or three-masted vessel with a raised deckhouse aft for living quarters and a pilot house for steering. Although these ships carried sails to steady them and for propulsion in a good breeze, they were designed to be towed, not to sail by themselves. They usually had a crew of three, as one man was always needed at the wheel. The companies did not maintain them very well and they often were overloaded; some carried as much as 3,500 tons, equal to the capacity of the larger coastal schooners.

Schooner-barges were the most economical way to move bulk cargo, and thus they were ideal for transporting coal. They sailed the coast in great numbers. A seagoing tugboat would string out three or four of them for a mile or more, with a single heavy tow rope between them. As a result they were a danger at night and in fog, because other skippers could not know how long the tow was. Steering was often directed from the tugboat by whistle signals, as the master could not see the last barges, they were so far astern. Extra tugboats, stationed at Vineyard Haven, kept the barge fleets on schedule around the cape. The port had been used long before the canal, and most of the tugboats made it their home port throughout the 1920s. That kept the coal moving around the cape and was a major reason the Cape Cod Canal was losing money.

In the fall of 1917 America's war effort finally took its toll on the canal business. The United States Navy bought the three steamers of the Eastern Steamship Lines, the *Old Colony*, the *Bunker Hill*, and the *Massachusetts*, for conversion to military use. Their replacements were smaller ships, mostly from that line's Down East fleet.

Up to the time the canal opened, Belmont had indicated no interest in selling it to the federal government, although the *New York Times*, as early as August of 1914, suggested it might be a good idea. But Belmont changed his mind sometime in 1915. In Boston, the Board of Harbor and Land Commissioners looked into the possibility of the state's taking over the canal. Following the study they concluded it was not for the state to do, but rather for the federal government. Belmont agreed.

The secretary of the navy, Josephus Daniels, went through the canal on a navy vessel and then invited canal executives to a Washington, D.C. meeting. The get-together was not official, just exploratory, concerning the price and possible purchase of the canal by the federal government. Daniels said he thought the government should buy the waterway.

After the declaration of war, a bill was introduced in the United States Senate by Sen. John Weeks of Massachusetts calling for government purchase through negotiation or, if that failed, condemnation of the canal. An admiral said the canal had value because German U-boats were being reported off Martha's Vineyard and Nantucket. Federal steamboat inspectors were placed on ships using the waterway to see that no one blocked the channel through sabotage.

Under the Rivers and Harbors Act of 1917 three federal government departments—navy, war, and commerce—were to investigate the possibility of buying the canal, assessing its cash value and the need for improvements. Belmont approved "heartily" and agreed to do what he could "to further the matter." The Army Corps of Engineers was asked to assist, too. The accounting firm of Price, Waterhouse audited the Canal Company's books to determine actual cost of the waterway. It came up with a figure of $8,265,743.04 in construction costs to the day the canal opened, July 29, 1914. The completion of the canal and a stock bonus, plus operating losses, brought the total figure to $12,956,718.31 by August of 1917. The Army Corps of Engineers took the lower, 1914 figure, suggesting if the government were to purchase the canal it should not do so at a price "greater than $8,265,743.04." Another committee suggested a different figure. The River and Harbors Board of Engineers studied the audit and came up with $3.5 million as the value of the waterway to the public. But since Belmont had written in 1916 that the canal "is now being operated upon a profitable basis," the board decided against buying it as the owners "are satisfied with the present situation." Nothing could have been further from the truth. The Canal Company wrote back saying that "we want the Government to take over the Canal, because . . . we cannot swing it." The board then submitted another report, recommending purchase by the federal government for $3.5 million. August Perry Belmont's bank was near shock when it received this figure.

But soon the federal government would be inspired to raise its ante. The Imperial German Navy had several submarines roaming the East Coast of the United States in May of 1918, causing little damage but quite a bit of fear. A number of vessels that were formerly strangers to the cut through Cape Cod started using it for protection from attack. On the morning of July 21, a German submarine, the *U-156*, spotted a tugboat and tow several miles off Chatham. The warship surfaced and started firing a deck gun at the tugboat, the *Perth Amboy*, and her four barges. The tugboat was burned out but not destroyed; the barges sank.

The next day Pres. Woodrow Wilson ordered the secretary of war, Newton D. Baker, to have the Federal Railroad Administration, already running the country's trains, take over and operate the canal. Four days later the government was in charge. The waterway was in bad physical condition; the channel had been allowed to shoal up so badly that in places there were only seventeen feet of water instead of twenty-five. The banks were badly eroded, while some dolphins were deteriorating and others were missing. An improvement program began.

The chief of the Army Corps of Engineers turned in a report to Secretary Baker a few days later, calling the canal a "necessity" to the war effort and suggesting the federal government buy it for $10 million and enlarge it to a 200-foot channel, thirty feet deep. In November of 1918, President Wilson wrote the secretaries of commerce, war and navy, asking them to "proceed with the business" of purchasing the Cape Cod Canal as it is "from every point of view desirable that we should acquire" it. Wilson's attitude was no surprise, as he had also favored government purchase of the privately owned Chesapeake and Delaware Canal, linking the upper reaches of those two bays. That purchase took place in 1919 for $2.5 million.

The federal government offered the Canal Company $8,250,000 for the Cape Cod Canal. When the company refused the offer, condemnation proceedings were started in the Federal District Court at Boston. The government ran the canal from July 25, 1918, to March 1, 1920, collecting the same tolls as were in effect when it took over, although it permitted the railroads to raise their rates over one-fourth because of war-induced inflation. The deficit for the canal during the government's nineteen-month operation was $739,620.30 excluding interest on the bonds. The working day had been shortened from twelve to eight hours, while salaries were raised and the number of employees more than doubled. Two major items in the loss were dredging, which cost $285,000, and a revived and expanded tugboat service of eight vessels, which in 1919 alone lost $200,000.

The canal was generally improved by government ownership. It was dredged to proper depth, including the western approach nearly five miles into Buzzards Bay. A number of dolphins were replaced, though not all that needed to be, and almost ten thousand tons of small stone were laid as riprap along the decaying banks. The losses incurred were paid by the federal government.

Sen. Henry Cabot Lodge of Massachusetts wrote a bill in 1919 to buy the canal, but when the bill reached the Committee on Commerce he changed it into a compensation arrangement. It failed to pass.

In October, the condemnation trial started in Boston before a jury charged with fixing a value for the thirteen-mile waterway. The Canal Company lined up a parade of impressive witnesses, including Gen. George W. Goethals, chief engineer for construction of the Panama Canal. He testified that at 1919 prices the Cape Cod Canal would cost about $28 million to build if the government did the work, or as much as $40 million if it were done privately. The company claimed total costs of $14,710,816.05 up to the day the Federal Railroad Administration took over in July of 1918. The figure was challenged, since some of it was not cash paid out, but included stock in the Canal Company, stock that was used only as a bonus for other purchases and never sold outright.

The attorney for the Boston, Cape Cod and New York Canal Company, Sherman L. Whipple, emphasized the value of the waterway to national defense. While admitting the canal was losing money, he said this was because it was still being developed. He made one point over and over: the federal government had initiated the moves to take over the canal.

The federal government's case was handled by Nathan Matthews, a former Boston mayor. He argued that while the canal was perhaps a necessity during the German submarine offensive, its value to the overall national defense was not great. As a franchise, he said, it had no value, since it was losing money.

The Canal Company had tried to convince the jury there was great traffic potential that would increase the value of its property. To do this it called in a transportation expert, Prof. Emory R. Johnson of the University of Pennsylvania, who testified concerning his traffic projections. Matthews called these merely conjecture. He claimed the cost of the canal was less than $8 million "of money actually and reasonably spent."

While conceding sincerity to Belmont in constructing the waterway, Matthews said its builders had long considered dumping their losses on the government, an idea contained in the confidential prospectus of 1907. It was a bad business investment, said Matthews, and the people of the United States had no stake in bailing out its promotors.

Matthews asked the jury for a "just verdict for the amount of the present value of this property." His adversary, Whipple, asked for $25 million.

The judge charged the jury "to decide the fair market value of the Cape Cod Canal." That same day, November 18, 1919, the jury made its decision. To it the canal was worth $16,801,201.11. A simultaneous verdict gave the government $150,000 on its suit to recover the $400,000 spent to improve the waterway after the Federal Railroad Administration took over. (Costs of dredging in Buzzards Bay, under federal domain, remained in the government's hands.) The judge's decree was delayed until the following year, as was the appeal by the government on a writ of error.

The Federal Railroad Administration tried to return the canal to its owners on March 1, 1920. Belmont would not accept it, since it had gone through condemnation trial brought by the federal government and a verdict had been handed down. So far as he was concerned, the canal was government property, and, although there had been no judgment by the court, the government would run it. On orders from Belmont's New York office, the canal was closed.

For many areas it was a bad time. Fuel supplies in northern New England were short, and rail delivery was slow because of heavy snow. The governor of Massachusetts, Calvin Coolidge, wired the War Department to take over and operate the canal; the request was refused. Ships were beginning to fill anchorages at both ends, waiting. A few went around the cape. Coolidge then pleaded with the Canal Company, which reluctantly agreed to reopen the waterway, while insisting it was now federalized by the court action.

On the morning of March 4 employees of the Canal Company were back at work and soon a fleet of eastbound barges, carrying coal and oil, passed through the waterway like a parade. Off Sandwich, westbound ships were anchored or tied to dolphins, waiting. As most of them were light, they had the lowest priority for passage.

Capt. Harold L. Colbeth had become superintendent of the canal in

1917, succeeding Capt. Edward Redding Geer, who, like his old boss Jacob W. Miller, had come from the Fall River Line. Colbeth had served the Federal Railroad Administration and was the obvious choice to run the waterway for the interim period, which the company thought would be brief. At that point, in the winter of 1920, no one could have forseen the future—that the Boston, Cape Cod and New York Canal Company would be running the waterway for the next eight years.

The company did two things that year to show a profit—increased tolls by one-fifth and spent nothing on maintenance. More than eighty-one hundred ships paid $357,000 against expenses of $182,000, producing a surplus of almost $175,000. That did not include, of course, the $300,000 interest on the bonds or the loans made to Belmont that were renegotiated frequently; the canal would have had to net a half-million dollars to cover those. But for the first time it at least took in more money than it paid out in operating costs.

On August 20, 1920, the judge who had heard the case entered the decree, allowing the company to ask Congress to appropriate the amount set by the jury to buy the waterway. The federal government appealed on September 30. In February of 1921 the First Circuit Court of Appeals in Boston granted the writ of error sought by the government, returning the case to the court. If the company and the government could not have agreed on a price, a new trial would have been necessary.

In the meantime, the chief of the Army Corps of Engineers had one of his best people, Col. Edward Burr, begin a thorough study of the history and operation of the canal. Secretary of War Baker, calling the jury's verdict "grossly excessive," wanted much more information than the federal government presented for its case during the first trial. Burr began his investigation in February of 1921. His report stated that the government should buy the waterway, enlarging it to a 200-foot channel with a depth of thirty-five feet, and install a single set of locks to control the current.

While Burr was making his study, the parties agreed to negotiate. Calvin Coolidge was now the vice president of the United States, and another Massachusetts man, former Sen. John W. Weeks, was the new secretary of war. In addition to this influence, State Sen. Charles H. Innes—the single most powerful man in Massachusetts politics, with the ear of all its congressmen—was a close friend of H. P. Wilson, the vice president of the Canal Company. On July 29, 1921, August Perry Belmont signed a contract with the government to sell the canal for $11.5 million. The agreement was with Weeks, who, as secretary of war, had been empowered to negotiate through the Rivers and Harbors Act of 1917. The federal government was to pay

$5.5 million in cash and take responsibility for the interest and eventual payment of the $6.0 million in bonds.

For its part the Canal Company had to turn over the canal with a channel twenty-five feet deep; the 932 acres owned by the Construction Company were to be included with the purchase, and a balance of $100,000 was required in the bank at the time of the transaction. Until approval by Congress, which also would have to appropriate the money, the Canal Company had to operate the waterway and pay its expenses.

On December 12, 1921, Rep. Samuel E. Winslow of Massachusetts introduced a bill in Congress to purchase the canal under the terms agreed to by Belmont and Weeks. At first passage of the bill seemed assured as House Speaker Frederick H. Gillette of Massachusetts sent it to the Committee on Interstate and Foreign Commerce, whose chairman was Winslow. But the hearings seemed endless, and finally in May of 1922, Winslow wrote another bill that contained all the provisions of the first one, except that it provided for the company to waive claims against the Federal Railroad Administration. That bill sailed through committee with a recommendation to the full House that it be passed.

In the Senate, Henry Cabot Lodge of Massachusetts introduced a similar bill, and the Commerce Committee included it as an amendment to its annual rivers and harbors bill. This passed the Senate but required a conference, as the canal purchase was a separate House bill, not part of the Rivers and Harbors Act for that year. The conference thought $9 million an appropriate price, but the canal supporters rejected it. The Senate accordingly dropped the canal purchase amendment and for that session the matter was dead.

The number of ships using the canal in 1921 and 1922 dropped to around seven thousand for each year; income averaged $345,000 yearly, with expenses up in 1921 and down in 1922, producing a two-year profit of $330,000.

As previously noted, before the canal had been built the promoters believed coastal tows would provide much of its business and perhaps even be its largest single source of revenue, but most of that trade was still using Pollock Rip Channel. Now a new development in shipping was seen more and more in the canal, as box barges of shallow draft brought coal north and transported granite south. Requiring only one crew member on each barge, they were far cheaper to operate than the large schooner-barges of coastal tows. They became important carriers, and their owners were given insurance on trips to northern New England when they used the protected route the canal afforded. Although the box barge boom helped canal finances, money problems persisted—there just was not enough business. Only 20 percent of the ships that could use the canal did so, and their numbers continued to decline. In 1923 the tolls were raised again and the surplus reached $276,500. Income dropped in 1924 with 1,100 fewer ships having used the canal, but a reduction in expenses, including nearly 50 percent less dredging, produced a net profit of $273,000. Ship passages dropped by more than five hundred in 1925, expenses rose, and the surplus sank to $169,000.

The legislative news during this period was no better. Winslow had introduced his bill for the second time and it had passed his House Commerce Committee in February of 1924. That May, when it reached the House floor, two amendments that would have reduced the price for the canal were defeated. The bill finally passed by a vote of 150 to 131, with almost as many congressmen not voting as had voted for the bill. Approval was now up to the Senate, where the bill did not get through the Commerce Committee until late January of 1925. When a senator from Maine tried to put the Cape Cod Canal bill into the Rivers and Harbors Act as an amendment, the move was tabled by a close vote.

Far from the political maneuverings in Washington, D.C., and the financial frustrations of August Perry Belmont and his New York office was the day-to-day operation of the canal. It had been a ship-watchers mecca since its opening, and in June of 1924, it became more popular than ever for Cape Cod natives and visitors. Two new white steamers—sister ships, the *Boston* and *New York*—began daily service between their namesake cities, replacing the smaller vessels that Eastern Steamship Lines had used on the summer runs ever since the navy bought the three original steamers in 1917. The "New York boat" was the passage that attracted the crowds. Leaving India Wharf in Boston at 5 P.M., she reached the Sandwich entrance to the canal around 8 P.M. and with a fair tide was at Bournedale twenty minutes later. People would walk or drive to their favorite spots to see her glide through the narrow cut. It was the equivalent of going down to the depot to see the train come in, a popular social exercise in many other towns. And each night a mystical, stately tribute was paid the great ship as she cut through the canal's inky waters. Ten-year-old Gilbert S. Portmore had moved with his family to Gray Gables, and it was there that he waited for the "New York boat" to pass. Faithfully, as she reached State Pier, young Gil raised his bugle and sounded taps through the summer air. In reply, the ship's captain would blast his whistle three times and raise and lower his searchlight. World War II spelled the end of the love affair. Gil went off to serve as a fighter pilot; he returned, but was killed in 1944 in a Kentucky plane crash. The *New York* was sunk in 1942, along with her sister ship, by German submarines while on the way to Ireland.

A popular postcard on the cape carried a poem, "The New York Boat," in which Marjorie Bassett immortalized the canal-watchers' experience.

> *Have you ever been down by*
> *the Cape Canal*
> *When the New York boat*
> *went through?*
> *Of all the sights I love so well*
> *That one is ever new.*
>
> *It's fun to ride along awhile*
> *Then to stop by the*
> *bank to wait.*
> *It's fun to watch the folks*
> *arrive*
> *Some early and some late.*

> *Now if you've never been there*
> *To see that boat go by,*
> *You've missed a sight beyond*
> *compare,*
> *I'm going to tell you why.*
>
> *At dusk the old Cape Cod*
> *Canal*
> *Takes on a glamorous hue*
> *And 'tis a glorious spot at*
> *which to dwell*
> *While the New York boat*
> *goes through.*

The "Boston boat," coming east, was not quite so popular. She reached Wings Neck Light about 5:00 A.M. and while many passengers made it to the deck to see the canal, their numbers were not matched by those along the shore. Overall, though, the ships were instantly popular, and the total number of passengers traveling the canal in 1924 jumped to 133,000 from the previous year's 116,000. The following year the number broke 160,000. The S.S. *Boston* was in service a little over one month when her career almost ended after a collision in cottonlike fog off Rhode Island. She was towed to Newport and, after considerable repairs, returned to the run later that summer.

The new steamers finished their first season in November and were laid up in East Boston for the winter. In Washington, D.C., the Massachusetts politicians were planning their strategy, for the canal bill was soon to be considered by the Senate's Commerce Committee. In his New York office, on December 9, 1924, Belmont had been having pains in his arm for much of the day. When the pain increased, his son Morgan took him home. Following emergency surgery for blood poisoning, he rallied, then lost ground. The next evening, December 10, August Perry Belmont died. He was seventy-one. His canal, never easy for him but seldom uninteresting, was ten years old.

Belmont's lifetime record of success, particularly in transportation, had fallen with the Cape Cod Canal. He approached the canal with the Midas touch; it turned to lead. Belmont had put more money into the canal than anyone, and he lost about $1 million in cash on his original investment. His actual loss was about $5 million—the amount he could have earned by investing his $1 million elsewhere. When he died, after spending eighteen years of his life on the project, Belmont left behind a crumbling dream, a waterway even the spendthrift federal government did not want.

Though Calvin Coolidge became president after the death of Warren G. Harding in 1923, this did not help advance the canal legislation the former Massachusetts governor favored. A month before Belmont died, Coolidge won the presidency on his own. In his message to Congress in January of 1925, he asked for passage of a canal bill. After it failed in the Senate, he repeated his request a year later and within a short time a bill was introduced in the House. This time it was assigned to the Rivers and Harbors Committee. Six months later, in June of 1926, the House passed a rivers and harbors act that included purchase of the canal. The Senate began debating it on December 6 with the support of New England members—and the usual opposition from some areas of the Middle West. Following the Christmas recess, the bill passed the Senate on January 21, 1927. Finally.

According to provisions of the bill, the government would pay $5.5 million in cash for the canal and assume responsibility for the $6.0 million in bonds and the interest on them from the day canal ownership was transferred. To provide the necessary monies, Congress approved an appropriations act for $50 million, part of which would be used for purchasing the canal. Or so it was believed. As it turned out, there was no money in the act to make the cash payment, and it was not until just before Christmas that a bill was passed to provide it.

After the land titles had been verified, the United States attorney general wrote the secretary of war, informing him the canal belonged to the federal government, and the Army Corps of Engineers took over the property at 12:00 P.M. on March 31, 1928. The employees of the Canal Company were happy to learn that nothing would change for them; they would continue to work, but for a different boss, Uncle Sam.

Since 1926 ship traffic through the canal had climbed slightly to 5,259 vessels, with the passenger total rising to 166,787. Income was up but so were expenses, and the surplus was $166,800, slightly less than the year before. In 1927 traffic rose by over five hundred vessels, with Eastern Steamship Lines adding two winter boats for year-round service between New York and Boston. That last full year of private ownership saw income reach its peak: $511,000. But the surplus was almost identical with that of the previous year—$166,658—as expenses for dredging to reach the twenty-five-foot depth requirement pushed total spending to $344,200, the highest under company management.

The agreement with the federal government required the company to have $100,000 in the bank on transfer of the title. Because there was less than that, it was agreed that the sale price should be reduced by that amount, making the actual cost $11.4 million.

There were people who believed the owners paid a high-pressure lobby to help them dump their fishy fiasco onto a pliant federal government, thereby making a huge profit. In his article, "Please Buy Wall Street's White Elephant," in *The Nation* of January 7, 1925, Arthur Warner called the canal's finances "a calamitous affair." Warner added, "The company is in a hole by comparison with which its own ditch across Cape Cod is only a scratch in the sand." Warner berated the newspapers for not identifying the Cape Cod Canal with August Belmont and Company nor with Secretary Weeks (a former banker), adding, "nor have they explained that the bill before Congress makes a present of $5,500,000 to a group of financiers who have no chance of getting a cent of that amount by operating the canal themselves." Warner's solution: "These men ought to be glad to deed the waterway to the government if it would take over their $6,000,000 bond issue, thus saving them further out-of-pocket expenses for interest not earned by the canal."

The criticism is only partially true. There had been a well-paid lobby for many years, but no one ever made money by investing in the Cape Cod Canal. Belmont's losses could be estimated as high as $5 million. Flanagan, the man who got the 1899 charter under which the canal was built, also lost money; he recovered only about forty percent of his $625,000. Those who held Canal Company stock received every cent they paid for it—nothing.

Three and one-half years after the government federalized the waterway, the stockholders or their heirs had a final meeting at an attorney's office in Boston. They voted unanimously to dissolve the Boston, Cape Cod and New York Canal Company. Three months later a court granted their petition.

4

Uncle Sam Takes Over

THE Army Corps of Engineers knew it was taking over a waterway that needed improvements, primarily a far wider and slightly deeper channel, with perhaps a lock to control the current. Colonel Burr's study of 1921–22 had recommended all these refinements. A dredging program was started in September of 1928 and those dolphins still in disrepair were replaced. More studies and surveys would be made, continuing a centuries-old tradition of the canal.

With tolls now eliminated all kinds of ships were attracted to the waterway, and in 1928 a record number of 9,312 vessels used the canal. Some of the greatest rejoicing took place at the headquarters of the Eastern Steamship Lines, which had been paying $1,500 per day for its two daily boats to pass through the waterway.

Still, the corps wanted more shipping. In January of 1929, a questionnaire mailed to companies shipping along the New England coast inquired: What is the matter with the Cape Cod Canal and why do not your ships use it? The answers were not surprising: narrow channel, swift currents, fear of collision with bridges, one-way traffic, vapor, and, for ships with low power, the need to wait for a favoring tide.

Through studies and public hearings the corps came up with expansion ideas that would increase the channel's width to 200 feet, its surface to 300 feet, its depth to thirty feet. With those dimensions, the canal could offer two-way traffic. Of course, some suggested a still larger waterway and a lock or two to control the current; indeed, the district engineer in charge of the canal, Col. S. A. Cheney of the New England Division, wanted locks. His plan called for a 300-foot-wide channel down the isthmus, with thirty-five feet of water and a 1,000-foot-long lock with twin chambers.

With a canal of that size in the works, the three bridges spanning it would have to be replaced by far larger structures. In the case of the highway bridges, they had to be high, fixed structures so that all vessels could pass beneath them, eliminating the draws that many mariners feared and allowing road traffic to cross continuously. This last point was important as automotive traffic was often backed up for some distance, especially in the summer. Replacement of the New Haven Railroad's bridge would be a more difficult undertaking. A high fixed bridge for trains would require the railroad to build the track up for miles with steep grades. Trains would then have to be broken up to get them across. The corps decided to erect a vertical lift bridge with one huge span that would ride up and down on towers, using counterweights. A mere seven feet would separate the span when it was lowered from the high waterline, so the corps decided to keep the span open, lowering the tracks only when a train approached.

At first plans called for one new highway bridge in the middle of the eight-mile isthmus. Local citizens were as totally opposed to that as they had been to the single drawbridge that Belmont's engineers had suggested in 1907, before the waterway was begun. Parsons had altered his plans to include two bridges; the Army Corps of Engineers did likewise. Their sites would remain near the old Bourne and Sagamore bridges. Federal money became available under the National Industrial Recovery Act of 1933 to build three new bridges (one railroad bridge and two highway bridges) and widen the channel in two stages to reach 205 feet. The act allotted $4.6 million. The highway bridge work began in early December of 1933, and both bridges opened for traffic following their dedications on June 21, 1935. Each bridge has a main span of 616 feet, with a clearance of 135 feet above high water. The railroad bridge was started a few weeks after the highway bridges. Construction took longer as cofferdams—waterproof underground compartments—were sunk to build supports for its twin towers. These had to carry a 540-foot span, the longest in the world at that time. The bridge weighs 2,050 tons and carries a single track. In those years of economic depression, more than seven hundred men were employed in four shifts of bridge work. On December 27, 1935, the first train rolled across the new bridge.

Another problem facing mariners using the canal was the approach channel up Buzzards Bay, with its two bends. The Army Corps of Engineers replaced this channel with a straight channel into Buzzards Bay above Hog and Mashnee islands. To prevent silt deposits and cross currents from the old channel, a two-mile dyke was built westward from Stony Point on the north and the two islands at the south end were connected to each other and the cape by a causeway. The causeway was built from material dredged from the new channel, a convenient and inexpensive means of construction. This new entrance, Hog Island Channel, is 4.7 miles long and 500 feet wide. Farther out, connecting with that section, is Cleveland Ledge Channel, 4.1 miles in length and 700 feet wide. The new Cape Cod Canal totals 17.4 miles; the Belmont canal was 13.0 miles long.

The corps decided to abandon the idea of locks and to retain an open canal after bitterly cold weather in two successive winters—1933 to 1934 and

1934 to 1935—clogged Buzzards Bay with ice. The canal did not freeze because of the current, but the planned lock near Sagamore Bridge would have stilled the water and allowed it to freeze, a much trickier situation for icebreakers than breaking through the wide water of the bay.

In December of 1934, a plan forwarded to Congress recommended an open waterway with a depth of thirty-two feet and a channel width down the isthmus of 540 feet. Better lighting, relocation of roads, mooring basins on either end, and a branch from the main channel into Onset Bay on the west so that small craft could use the bay as a port of refuge, along with the canal widening were part of the master plan approved in the Rivers and Harbors Act of August of 1935. Excavation in the lower cut began in the dry, parallel to the existing canal, with heavier riprap laid on the banks. The dry digging worked inward while dredges deepened the channel and then worked outward to the dry section. The new canal required removing 40 million cubic yards of material; the Belmont project had excavated 16 million cubic yards. The engineer of the new project reduced the channel width to 480 feet in the isthmus, giving an easier slope on the sides underwater. The slight reduction in width has never presented any problem in maintaining two-way traffic.

Making the improvements took a long time because the canal remained open during reconstruction, except for brief periods. When the improvements were completed in June of 1940, their total cost had reached $19.6 million. Labor was cheap during those depression years; the program could have been completed sooner, but men were used whenever possible in preference to machinery. A cardinal rule for public works projects during those tough times was to use as many of the unemployed as possible.

With the enlarged waterway, cargo tonnage climbed to 7,901,182 in 1940, up from 2,627,376 tons in 1935. The number of ships using the canal averaged a little over 11,000 per year through 1935, reaching 15,000 in 1940.

The change in passenger traffic during the renovation was not so fortunate. In 1927, the last full calendar year the canal remained in private ownership, 203,249 people traveled through it. That fall the Eastern Steamship Lines decided to make its New York-Boston service daily year-round. The S.S. *New York* and the S.S. *Boston* had been designed for summer service, with exposed lower decks and high, flat sides that made them especially vulnerable to high seas and heavy winds. But the line had acquired two big ships ideally suited for the stormy winter weather of the cape. It began placing those ships on the winter run while the S.S. *New York* and the S.S. *Boston* were spruced up at their berths at East Boston, then moving them to the Norfolk run when the original steamers returned in the spring. The year-round rotation continued until World War II. Passenger service peaked in

1930, with 248,200 people making the run. The next three years saw an annual drop, to 165,950 passengers in 1933. The trend reversed itself, climbing to 243,134 passengers by 1937. But in 1941, the last year of regular service, the total number of passengers had decreased to 175,373. World War II killed off not only the New York-Boston runs of the Eastern Steamship boats, but those of two other companies, the Merchants and Miners Line and the Savannah Line.

In the fall of 1939, some British ships in camouflage began using the canal to avoid German submarines. Although United States' active participation was two years away, the war came early to Cape Cod in the form of ships with deck guns and gray paint. Such ships gave very little information when hailed, often just the name of the coastal pilot. Some American industries were gearing for war through production of materials under the Lend-Lease agreement with Great Britain; and some of their products moved east through the canal in ships of British registry.

Four months before Pearl Harbor, Pres. Franklin D. Roosevelt was on his way to a meeting with British Prime Minister Winston Churchill in the harbor at Argentia, Newfoundland—a meeting that would produce the Atlantic Charter. Because of the threat of German U-boats sinking Churchill's ship, the H.M.S. *Prince of Wales*, as well as the danger to Roosevelt's life if the Nazis knew of the intended six-day meeting, the tightest security had to be maintained. Later, the head of the United States Secret Service said he did not know where the President had been for several days. On August 3, Roosevelt sailed from New London, Connecticut, on the yacht *Potomac*. It appeared to be a pleasure cruise Down East, but off Martha's Vineyard Roosevelt moved to the cruiser U.S.S. *Augusta*. With the chief executive rounding the cape on that vessel, the *Potomac* headed for Cleveland Ledge Channel and Buzzards Bay. Three sailors dressed to look like President Roosevelt, his press secretary, Steven Early, and his military aide, General Watson, lounged near the stern in comfortable chairs befitting those in the upper stations of life that August of 1941. The *Potomac* moved eastward through the canal and far into Cape Cod Bay with the three on deck for the entire passage. The hoax worked, as the talk along the canal and in nearby towns was of "seeing the President on his yacht."

With America's declaration of war on December 8, the United States Coast Guard assumed responsibility for the canal's operation and security. The other services were also included: coast and antiaircraft assignments were the responsibility of the army, while sea patrols fell to the navy. Operation headquarters were moved from Buzzards Bay to the Coast Guard Station at Sandwich. A port director's office was set up at Woods Hole to supervise the assembly of convoys bound for ports in Nova Scotia and Great Britain. Outside the mine fields the navy had placed to deter submarines, Buzzards Bay became a major anchorage for merchant vessels with war cargo. Soon vessels with bombers and tanks loaded on deck were commonplace among the tankers as the area south of Cleveland Ledge Light filled with ships forming another convoy. The vessels had come up the coast on their own; they would leave in single file up the mine-swept Cleveland Ledge and Hog Island channels into the land cut and be escorted from Cape Cod Bay up to Halifax, other convoy assembly ports, or directly across the Atlantic.

The largest ships had to be sent outside the cape, but most vessels could go through the canal. Some needed more water under their keels and so had to be run through the waterway around high tide, making tight scheduling crucial for convoys. One ship every 2,000 yards was the plan, a good one if every ship were the same—same power, same load, same size—and if the currents in the canal were constant. (Triple spacing was used for ships carrying ammunition and petroleum.) But there were considerable differences in ships, the experience of crews, their knowledge of the canal, and the changing phases of tides and the currents, all making the naval close order drills somewhat harrowing.

Overall, though, it worked out surprisingly well. Only one serious accident occurred in the land cut during the war—the sinking of a collier some seven months after the Japanese attack on Pearl Harbor. The vessel, the S.S. *Stephen R. Jones*, was a regular out of Boston, hauling bituminous coal (it was not in convoy). The *Jones* took a sheer and hit the north bank of the canal less than one-half mile east of Bourne Bridge. She damaged her plates forward and sank by the bow. Salvage efforts failed and she settled into the bottom, blocking the canal totally. Shades of the S.S. *Bayport* in 1916! It was decided to remove the *Jones* the same way—with dynamite. Thirty-four days and sixty-seven explosions later, the S.S. *Stephen R. Jones* and her 7,000 tons of coal were spread around the channel bottom and the canal reopened. The area gouged out of the north bank of the canal by water forced up around the hull is still visible, and ships' compasses still become jumpy and erratic when vessels pass the spot. The possibility of sabotage was investigated, but that was a really silly probe, for there was no question of the loyalty of those aboard the unfortunate ship. The *Jones* simply hit the bank when she took a sheer—an accident that has happened to a number of vessels using the canal, but with such dire consequences to only two. During demolition, the convoys went outside the cape and one ship was lost. Six days after the *Jones* sank, a rerouted freighter was torpedoed and sunk east of the cape; ten of her crew were lost.

Two years later seven men were killed when a destroyer collided in the canal with a smaller vessel used to board convoy vessels. And in the final year of the war, 1945, two merchant ships collided far down Buzzards Bay. Only one sank, but the death toll was the worst—twenty-one people drowned —of any canal-related accident.

The traffic load and the pressure of work was intense during those years, with cargo tonnage up the first full calendar year, 1942, to 18,690,255 from 10,867,060 the year before. In 1943, cargo tonnage was 16,513,260 and in 1944, 18,851,194—the record year for the Cape Cod Canal.

There was considerable movement of personnel when convoys, containing as many as eighty ships, were sailing. Two coastguardsmen boarded each ship—one went to the bridge, the other next to the steering engine. They were taken off after the ship cleared the waterway. Traffic was one-way and eastbound (loaded) convoys had priority. For safety, many large, empty ships returning from Europe went west through the canal; they were too deep to transit when loaded, but the safety of the route gave them a better chance of survival when they were unloaded. A sad sight during those years was the torpedo victims still afloat and under tow—holes in their sides, fire-blackened, some listing badly, shattered steel topside, occasionally with a bow blown out.

The steamers *Boston* and *New York* and their "Honeymoon Convoy" of East Coast overnight steamers from Long Island Sound and Chesapeake Bay went east early in September of 1942. Gone was their white paint, replaced by navy gray. Their lower decks were covered as protection against the Atlantic. No waving passengers this time, no orchestras on the upper decks. It had been less than one year since they made their last trip as Eastern's best known New York to Boston boats—the symbols of the canal. Now a British merchant marine flag flew at the stern of each. Twenty-two days later, off the Irish coast, torpedoes sank them both.

Even before war had been declared the navy had been making plans for maximum use of the canal. As it turned out, the canal's greatest service was during those years, vindicating those who had praised its military value from as far back as the American Revolution. We can never know how many ships and liners were saved by its use, but the number must be large.

In November of 1945, the Coast Guard and the navy returned control of the canal to the Army Corps of Engineers, which continues to operate and maintain it. Passenger service is gone except for an occasional cruise ship adding a scenic leg to its trip. Traffic rose steadily through the 1950s and 1960s, and today numbers between 30,000 and 32,000 vessels annually, of which 6,500 are cargo ships carrying 13.5 million tons, mainly petroleum. Fuel is still the major coastal cargo entering northern New England, and most of it passes through the canal. Besides freighters carrying general merchandise, other types of cargo vessels, such as container ships with aluminum boxes stacked on deck, are common on the canal.

Earlier, canal promoters had talked and written of "the great commercial opportunity" to follow completion of the waterway; such visions were a regular part of the speeches of Belmont and Miller. But those visions were never realized. The largest industry in the vicinity of the canal, the Keith Car and Manufacturing Company, was in Sagamore long before the waterway was built, and that firm closed in the late 1920s. The only commercial development to be attached to the canal was a small fish-processing plant and an electric power plant, both located at Sandwich.

In 1948, the Massachusetts Maritime Academy moved from the state teachers' college it occupied at Hyannis to Taylors Point, along the canal at Buzzards Bay. The state had built a pier there in the early 1930s, dedicating it with a prophecy of Buzzards Bay becoming "one of the most important shipping and transfer points along the Atlantic seaboard." Ocean liners were also predicted to use the pier, as the location was "twelve hours nearer European ports." Because none of this has come about or is ever likely to, the Maritime Academy keeps its training ship—the 489-foot S.S. *Bay State*— tied to the pier most of the time. Once a year she sails with 600 cadets on an eight-week cruise to Europe. The school, with expanding facilities on fifty-five acres, contributes more to the local economy than any other single enterprise along the canal.

5

The Cape Cod Canal Today

ROBERT F. Smalley looks out over the Cape Cod Canal from the traffic control center. Before him is a U-shaped console, a battery of bright radar displays, closed-circuit television monitors, a two-way radio system, and an alpha-numeric display of data on tides and winds from three points along the waterway and from the hurricane barrier at New Bedford. This is the master control, where a marine traffic control officer is always on duty.

The center looks like an airport control tower, with uninterrupted runs of tinted glass forming the three exposed walls. From his post on the north bank of the canal a few hundred feet west of the rail bridge, Smalley gazes out on the *Ocean 250*, a huge oil barge heading west. She's light, with high, black sides giving her 546 feet the appearance of a huge, steel box. At her stern is a tugboat, the *Intrepid*, with a pilot house on a tripod seventy-one feet above the water. The height is needed to see over the barge, and an elevator is used to scale the tower. The *Intrepid's* bow is fitted into a notch in the stern of *Ocean 250* and held there hydraulically. Such a rig is called an integrated barge.

"We're getting an awful lot of barges of that size coming through here," Smalley says. "We have to have visibility of two miles throughout the canal. With so many ships of this size, when fog socks us in, we change to one-way traffic or we close the canal."

Of all the jobs performed at the canal by the seventy-five-man staff of the Army Corps of Engineers, the greatest responsibility falls on the seven marine traffic controllers, most of whom have moved up from the ranks of boatmen or deckhands. Working eight-hour shifts, often alone but occasionally in pairs, the traffic controllers must make instant decisions and then live with them. The job calls for a lot of personal judgment, judgment that comes only from long experience and intimate, personal knowledge of the entire length of the canal. Bob Smalley is one of the "junior" men. He has twenty-five years' service.

Even so, there are times when Smalley needs the help another man can provide.

The phones are ringing like mad. Ships' agents are calling. And it's a funny thing with the phone: when it rings you never know what it's going to be. It often means you have to take some action, make a decision. It could be a collision that someone else reports, a jumper—a suicide try from one of the bridges—a boat fire, a barge breaks loose from a tug, or a malfunction in the steerage. That's a common thing—a loss of steerage because of electrical failure. Of course we have to be terribly safety-conscious, and we are, but a malfunction in steerage we have no control over.

The job was made a bit more manageable with the installation in September of 1973 of a comprehensive television system. Ships within the 17.4 miles of the canal and approach channels, all under the jurisdiction of the traffic controller, are under constant surveillance while passing through the waterway, approaching it from either end, or clearing to deep water. "One thing about this new system," Smalley says, "it eliminates about 90 percent of the guess work. Now you can actually see the ships and make an intelligent decision. Before we had binoculars and no two-way radio. There were traffic stations then at Wings Neck and Sandwich as well as here. It was difficult, especially in bad weather." Now ten television monitors on the console show what the two cameras at each of five locations see. There are two cameras mounted on seventy-foot towers at Wings Neck and Sandwich to cover the approaches to the canal. One instrument is at a height of seventy feet; the other is at forty feet. Atop the two towers are radar scanners. Two cameras, one pointing east, the other west, are mounted high on the towers of the rail bridge. Peering around the two bends in the canal are camera sites at Station No. 259 on the south bank and at Station No. 160 on the north bank. Each of the ten cameras "hands off" pictures of every vessel to the next camera, permitting the traffic controller to see all the canal and past it to deep water. He can tilt, pan, zoom in or out, and focus each camera independently, and for a better look at a situation he can punch up any picture on one of two larger, thirty-inch monitors above the main console. Between them are four screens, showing tide stages and wind direction and velocity.

On his eight-hour shift a traffic controller can expect anything. The captains of big cargo vessels are in touch with him by radio. They call when they are outside the approach channels, giving their estimated time of arrival (ETA). To get priority positioning for the passage through the canal, which is usually reserved for government vessels and the big, loaded tankers, the captains of cargo vessels are often overly optimistic about their ETA.

During the summer, when small craft use the canal in great numbers, two patrol boats are in frequent service—often around the clock—as most pleasure boats do not have radios. Such craft, whose skippers are amateurs so far as water safety is concerned, can be a problem; "unbelievable" is the way traffic controllers put it. Sailboats are required to use their auxiliary power in the land cut and out in Buzzards Bay, too, if they continue in the channel there.

Within the canal, speed restrictions are important. A limit of ten miles per hour is enforced for small craft, which, if they have sufficient power, are permitted to enter the canal at any time unless specifically forbidden by traffic controllers. Vessels over twenty-five feet long, with or without radar, are cautioned not to transit until cleared by the traffic lights at either end of the canal, or by radio, radiotelephone, megaphone, or patrol boat. Minimum running times through the cut are thirty minutes with a fair tide, forty-five minutes with a slack tide, and one hour against a head tide. Time and speed regulations are enforced so a ship's wash will not endanger other vessels or damage banks. The television cameras have made strict enforcement of these regulations much easier.

Currents, a problem since the day the canal opened in 1914, result from the range of tides peculiar to the area. In Cape Cod Bay the mean tide range is 9.4 feet; in Buzzards Bay it is less than half that: only 4.0 feet. The phase and mean tide levels are also different in both bays, producing high tide in Buzzards Bay three hours and fifteen minutes ahead of that in Cape Cod Bay. The current changes direction about every six hours, although the eastward flow averages six hours and twenty-five minutes. The westward currents are more rapid because of the greater depth of high water at Sandwich than at Wings Neck. The top speed of the currents is 5.4 knots, or 7.6 feet per second. That, plus bends and bumps in the channel, can produce situations that tax even the most experienced mariner.

> At Bournedale [Smalley notes] in the bend of the canal there are tricky currents and eddies. A ship can easily take a sheer and go into the bank there. We've had it happen. The corps has these two tugs here for such emergencies. We can get a crew and move them out fast. In an emergency you've got to move fast. Instant decisions based on many factors, one of which is a memory reserve.

> We have a big oil barge that comes through, and she behaves strangely in the currents; it has something to do with the shape of her hull. Whenever she reaches that spot at the bend, she tends to sheer. We make sure she's in center channel and there's nothing near her coming the other way. You commit these things to memory. You have to.

The Cape Cod Canal Today | 75

The shifting tides and peculiar currents also create shoals, mostly of fine sand from within the canal itself. Dredging the channel clean is the major maintenance item in the corps budget—between 200,000 and 300,000 cubic yards of sand are removed each year. The Army Corps of Engineers operates a fleet of dredges to keep navigable rivers and harbors at their required depths. Once a year, usually in the spring, the hopper dredge *Comber* visits the canal; it operates as a hydraulic pump with a big pipe on the port side amidships, sucking up sand from the bottom and depositing it in tanks aboard ship. When these are filled to their capacity of 3,000 cubic yards, the *Comber* dumps the material in Cape Cod Bay or in lower Buzzards Bay. The shoaling areas within the land cut are short, usually from 100 to 200 feet long.

Water temperature presents another problem for traffic controllers. A daily reading of water temperature is taken at a little tide gauge house near the rail bridge. When the temperature reaches twenty-nine degrees and the forecast calls for continued cold weather, another factor becomes part of the center's decision-making calculus.

> The canal doesn't freeze over in the sense of being completely solid [Smalley notes]. In the land cut the ice gets broken from the ships, and the current moves it back and forth. When it's really cold, it piles up on top of each other in broken floes and gets thick. In a bad winter the ice is so thick it can stop a big ship. Then we have to get Coast Guard ice breakers. It has been so bad we have had to close the canal or run it one-way. We've even lost beacons sitting on cement legs, and the ice takes them right out. The legs, too. Sometimes the Coast Guard takes the buoys out, because of the ice. Then they'll use what they call an ice buoy, which can run under, rather than a bell or gong buoy. Buzzards Bay has on several occasions frozen over completely, but the current in the canal prevents its happening there.

As keeper of the government's land along the canal, the corps also encourages its use for recreational purposes, and ground along both banks is available at all times to fishermen. Catches of flounder, cod, bass, and mackerel are plentiful, with annual averages of more than sixty thousand pounds. Each year, more than 1 million persons visit the canal area. The Town of Bourne runs the Bourne Scenic Park on the north bank of the canal under a lease arrangement with the corps and has developed camp and picnic sites and a saltwater swimming pool along the shore. On the eastern end of the waterway, under another lease, the Massachusetts Department of Public Works operates the Scusset State Beach for swimming, picnicking, and pier fishing. However, fishing, lobstering, or trolling by boat are prohibited in the land cut between Cape Cod Bay and the State Pier.

The final main duty of the corps, in addition to traffic control, dredging, monitoring water temperature, and management of the recreation area is maintenance of the three bridges that span the canal. Routine expenses are paid out of the annual appropriation from the Rivers and Harbors Act. Painting, resurfacing decks, and replacing steel and cables are extra. The corps pays the quasi-governmental corporation, Conrail, to keep operators on the railroad bridge for the two trains that pass over it per day, Monday through Friday. Sometimes even those two daily trains cause a problem. The regulations, Smalley says, state that the rail bridge will not be lowered if a vessel is within one-half hour away from it. But once, he recalls,

> I had a ship that was over an hour away, so I gave them [the train] the railroad bridge. He got the bridge down and he had a malfunction; he couldn't get it back up. The bridge called me and said: "I can't get it up, and I don't know when I can get it up." And I was just about due for a change of tide. So I called the ship—it was a Coast Guard vessel— and told them what the conditions were. She turned around and backed out of there; everything worked out all right. If it had been a much bigger ship—say a large tanker and she was coming east—we'd have to put her in the west end mooring basin. We wouldn't want to, but if it's a lesser of two evils, we could do it. We have another basin on the east end. We use them when weather conditions warrant; when it's bad. For comfort sake we put ships in there when it gets rough out in the bays. There's a safety factor, too. They have to anticipate a day of waiting.

And when the biggest ships come through, the controllers can not live without the tide tables. At low tide the eight-mile land cut holds 690 million cubic feet of water; at high tide an extra 100 million cubic feet comes in, raising the canal's level four feet—important for large tankers that ride deep in the water. They are usually brought through an hour before high water so, if they strike bottom, the extra water will move them off easily. The powerful wash also means controllers must plan for some vessels to pass each other on the straightaway, rather than at one of the canal's two bends.

Smalley remembers the biggest ship he ever handled, a 780-foot Italian tanker.

> I can't remember her name [he says]. She was coming on fast, so I checked the tide table and it was a little too early for high water. I told her to slow down. She radioed the pilot association next door to us and

made arrangements. They have their own pilot boats, and one of them took off down Buzzards Bay and put him aboard at the midway buoy. He brought the tanker through just before high tide. I wouldn't want to handle a ship through here much larger than that. She was huge.

When you have a close one like that everything could change on you if the wind shifts direction or increases or the barometer drops once the ship is in the canal. You have to stay on top of things, be constantly aware of changing conditions before you make a decision. Then it's just like an aircraft. Once it reaches a position of no return and he's committed, you've got to be sure you made the right decision. Because then if any accident should happen, you are left holding the bag.

Newcomers to the canal—ships carrying liquid propane—can be even more dangerous than the big tankers, and they travel under their own set of rules. Smalley explains:

Their cargo is refrigerated at 237 degrees below zero. At that temperature the property of the metal changes, so the steel is brittle as glass, and you don't want them to even nudge anything even though they're double-skinned. You have to be careful when they come through here light, since they keep 50,000 barrels of propane on board to hold the temperature down. It's explosive and flammable stuff. Very dangerous. If they're towed on a hawser they must have a helper tug, and if they're integrated at the stern or have a tug alongside, we'll let them go through, providing it's a Coast Guard certified tug with adequate power. We're getting more of these, and it's a whole new ball game. We have to be as careful as we were during the war with a Navy "hot tow"—high explosives, shells, and bombs.

Smalley scans the radar screens and checks the numbers on gauges reporting the tides and winds. After checking each of the television monitors, he moves the controls that operate the upper camera at Wings Neck, sweeping over the water with it, then zooming in on a large, dark shape heading into Cleveland Ledge Channel. His finger punches a button and above him the picture appears on one of the larger screens. He studies it closely and finally nods his head, as if recognizing a friend. A teleprinter with weather information starts a rapid beat back of him along the wall. He pays no attention. He will check it in a few minutes, giving the Coast Guard Station at Chatham time to finish its report.

A green-hulled tanker, the *Raymond J. Bushey*, is passing under the rail bridge, moving west with a fair current. Smalley eyes the ship quickly, noting a red flag high, forward. "She's carrying gasoline," he explains. Another flag—this one's red and white—is whipping in the wind. "Got a pilot aboard, too." The *Bushey* is light and riding so high the curve at her bow below the painted waterline is out of the water. "A lot of times they will unload from these larger tankers and then run it into smaller ports. They taxi petroleum."

To the west the Army Corps of Engineers' tugboat *Nauset* is on the north side of the channel, working her way east. She has been doing hydrographic survey work down Buzzards Bay. The *Bushey* glides past, rolling some long bow waves that reach out and slap against the *Nauset*. They break in a white line along her black hull. Smalley has been watching this. Now Smalley glances at the television monitors and then at the tide and wind gauges. He pans the higher camera at Wings Neck, finding that big eastbound vessel again. The *Carol B. Ingram* is a little larger now on the big screen overhead. He knows when the *Intrepid* and the *Bushey* pass her farther out there is a lot of room. No problems.

He pans the highest camera on the north bank at Station No. 160, a position that allows him and the others to see around the bends in the canal to the east. He zooms the camera in on a tanker unloading at the electric plant on the south bank of the canal at Sandwich. "It's quite a thing to see a loaded tanker go in there," he says. "They use two tugs. It involves more problems for us in terms of our traffic, our timing. We can't relax until the tanker is out of the channel and tied up."

There are only a few clouds this bright afternoon. Visibility is maximum; wind, moderate. It has been the kind of eight-hour shift Smalley calls "a piece of cake." During the 8 A.M. to 4 P.M. shift not only does daylight make it easier, but the traffic is lighter. More commercial vessels use the canal at night—it is all a matter of when a ship clears port.

The radio breaks in. "*Intrepid* to two-one."

Smalley snatches the microphone from the desk in front of the console. "This is two-one, *Intrepid*."

"Roger, I just cleared the channel. We passed Wings Neck at 3:27. That's three-two-seven. I'm all set now."

Smalley squeezes a bar that opens his microphone and answers: "That's three-two-seven. Thanks, captain. Have a nice trip."

"Thank you very much."

Smalley puts the microphone down and walks several steps to the typewriter, then taps the figures on the same line he used to log the *Intrepid's* passage. All ships passing through must be logged like this. To help, a small maritime library of world shipping is kept on the console: *Lloyd's Register of Merchant Ships, Record of American Bureau of Shipping*, and *Merchant Marine House Flags and Stack Insignia*. The controllers get information from the merchant ships and other larger vessels through radio contact: name, owner, port of origin, destination, nature of cargo, and tonnage of cargo. A small, separate book of pertinent data on the "regulars" is maintained to save time.

The *Nauset* is now opposite the traffic control center about fifty feet from the shore; deck hands are at her bow and amidships with docking lines in hand. The powerful diesel tugboat moves slowly against a four-knot current toward her dock a couple of hundred feet to the left of the Administration Building. She turns to starboard and below an engine room telegraph clangs. She slows broadside to the current. Another clang and a white foamy wake boils from under her stern. The *Nauset* backs in.

On one of the large television monitors the *Intrepid* is pushing the *Ocean 250* southwest down Cleveland Ledge Channel. On a smaller monitor, with the other picture from Wings Neck, is the *Bushey*, still in Hog Island Channel.

It is a few minutes before 4 P.M. when Howard W. Hebblethwaite walks in and greets Smalley. Hebblethwaite will be in charge of traffic control until midnight. The two talk about conditions, with Smalley passing on information his replacement will need to know. On a board outside the central counter is a sign painted red with white lettering across the top: "Duty Marine Traffic Controller." Each man has a sign with his name on it with hooks to hang it up when he is on duty. Hebblethwaite posts his sign; Smalley removes his. The radio cuts in.

"Hello two-one. Hello two-one. This is the *Carole B. Ingram*. We're inbound for the Cape Cod Canal, passing Wings Neck."

Hebblethwaite picks up the microphone. "This is two-one."

1. The widest artificial waterway in the world today, the Cape Cod Canal is photographed here from a plane, looking west over Cape Cod Bay.

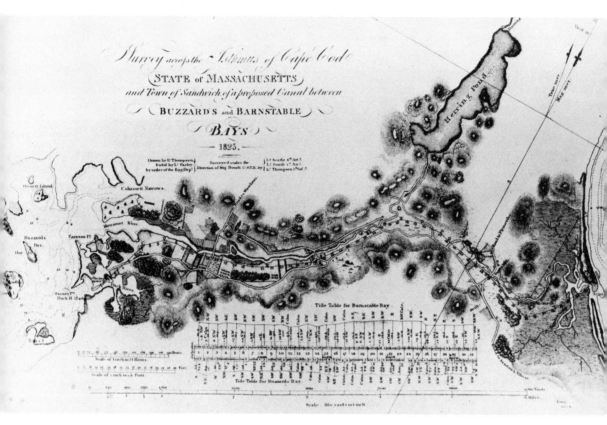

2. Major P. H. Perrault of the United States Army Corps of Engineers drew this map following his survey in the late fall of 1824. His route generally avoided the rivers, and on the eastern end included two possible entrances to the canal from Cape Cod Bay. One entrance was at Scusset Harbor and the other was about one mile north on dry ground.

(Opposite)
4. The Lockwood Dredge was the first mechanical device applied to digging the Cape Cod Canal. Towed to Sandwich in March of 1884, it was used, despite frequent breakdowns, until 1890, finishing a ditch almost 7,000 feet in length.

3. An old postcard view of some of the Italian "500" digging the Cape Cod Canal by hand was taken at Town Neck, Sandwich, in October of 1880. These workmen were never paid and—for the last few weeks they were there—never fed, at least by the company, which soon folded for lack of money.

(*Above*)

5. The *Hannah E. Shubert*, bound for Boston with a cargo of Pennsylvania coal, went aground on Peaked Hill Bars, Provincetown, March 9, 1886. She struck a shoal over one-quarter mile from shore, but heavy seas lifted her over the bars and onto the beach where her crew was rescued before a storm tore her to pieces.

(*Left*)

6. On April 11, 1888, the *Plymouth Rock* of Boston struck the Peaked Hill Bars at Provincetown and later at high tide with mountainous seas was lifted over them to the beach at the exact spot where the remains of the *Shubert* appear like so many tombstones in the sand. William P. Quinn, a marine historian whose specialty is shipwrecks, calls this "the classic wreck picture."

(*Above*)

7. Through wild seas and flying spray the crew of the British brig *Matilda Buck* reached the safety of the beach near Wood End Light, but their ship was pounded apart by the violent seas, after she struck shoals on January 9, 1890. In those days a wreck every two weeks was the Cape Cod average.

(*Below*)

8. The British bark *Kate Harding* was driven ashore at North Truro on Cape Cod by a violent northeast storm on November 30, 1892. The heavy surf carried her onto the sand with such force that her bottom was torn out. All ten crewmen were removed safely by breeches buoy.

9. Those aboard the full-rigged British ship *Jason* were not so lucky. *Jason* carried a crew of twenty-five men on her last voyage bound for Boston from Calcutta, India, with a cargo of jute. She was caught in a northeast gale off the Great Beach at Truro and driven onto a bar just off shore, where she was torn in half the evening of December 5, 1893. Only one man came out of that wild water alive.

(Left)
11. The *Walter Miller*, bound for New York with a cargo of Canadian lumber from St. John, New Brunswick, lost her way in dense fog and heavy seas on June 10, 1897, and wound up on Nauset Bar. Captain Barton, his wife, and the five crew members were brought ashore safely by breeches buoy, manned by a volunteer lifesaving crew. A tug pulled the ship free a few days later.

(Opposite)
10. The coal schooner *Charles A. Campbell* of New York made two unscheduled visits to Cape Cod's Great Beach. This is the first: March 14, 1894, at Truro. The surf appears to have been high enough to tear her rudder off, but it did not happen. Two days later the *Campbell* was towed off the shoals at high tide and she returned to the bituminous trade, sailing between Norfolk and New England coal ports. Eighteen years later she came ashore a bit farther down the coast near Wellfleet. Again, tugboats pulled her free. The *Campbell* has the beautiful lines of so many of her Down East sisters built in Maine shipyards, where she was born in Bath, "The City of Ships."

12. A lot of Canadian lumber destined for other places wound up in Cape Cod houses and other buildings because of shipwrecks. The *John S. Parker* made such a contribution to local construction on the night of December 7, 1901, when she was wrecked at Nauset Inlet. The *Parker*, like the *Walter Miller*, was bound for New York from St. John. The Life Saving Service brought the crew off safely with a breeches buoy. Wreckers salvaged some of the ship's cargo and sold it locally.

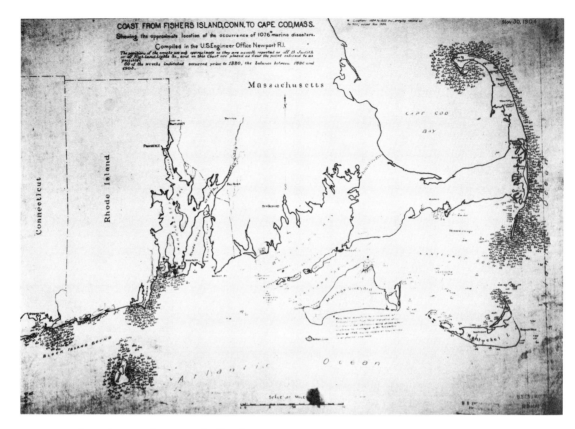

COAST FROM FISHERS ISLAND, CONN. TO CAPE COD, MASS.
Showing the approximate location of the occurrence of 1076 marine disasters.
Compiled in the U.S. Engineer Office Newport R.I.

Nov 30, 1904

13. The Army Corps of Engineers printed this map in 1904, showing all the known wrecks around Cape Cod and adjacent waters. August Perry Belmont had a copy framed on a wall of his New York office. The wrecks were printed in red ink. When she described this map in later years, Mrs. Belmont said, "The dots were so numerous one had the impression that red pepper had been sprinkled over the area."

(Opposite, bottom)
16. When a ship went aground or appeared to be in trouble, the nearest station sent its crew with a surfboat and beach apparatus for the breeches buoy. On Nauset Beach, life savers ran a breeches buoy out to a stranded vessel in this 1902 photograph taken by Buzzards Bay photographer Fred Small. These surfmen trained until they could fire a line to a ship and start rescue efforts within five minutes of reaching the beach. Although the greatest range for the Lyle Gun (which resembles a small mortar) was about 700 yards, the working limit was around 200 yards. At greater distances the current would carry the line away, or if it were secured, it would sag badly and subject a person carried to death from the pounding seas, immersion in cold water or drowning.

14. Despite the huge toll in lives and property, the United States government for many years did nothing besides build lighthouses and install other aids to navigation. It was left to the Massachusetts Humane Society to construct small huts along dangerous shores as shelters for shipwrecked sailors. Later the society erected lifeboat stations manned by volunteers. The United States Life Saving Service, created in 1849, did not serve Cape Cod until 1872, when it built and staffed nine stations like this one. Four more stations were added by 1900.

(Left)

15. Although sailing craft were more vulnerable in poor weather, steamers, too, had their share of accidents. The *Onondaga* grounded in heavy fog at Chatham, January 13, 1907. The cargo was removed to lighten her for refloating. For some Cape Codders rescue work provided a rare opportunity for winter employment—and more. When the steamship company checked the cargo brought out, it found $70,000 worth missing.

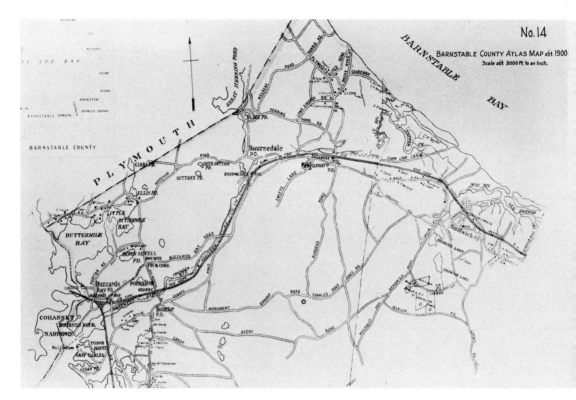

17. This 1900 map shows a proposed route of the Cape Cod Canal following the Monument River, until it turns north, and the New York, New Haven and Hartford Railroad. The river and the railroad shared the natural valley of the isthmus. Great Herring Pond, across the Plymouth County line, is the river's source. Lockwood's canal is indicated to the right.

18. The largest payroll on Cape Cod before the canal was built and for a dozen years after it opened was the Keith Car and Manufacturing Company of Sagamore. Isaac Keith founded the business in West Sandwich in 1846 to make carriages and stage coaches to be used in the opening of the West. The railway age presented even greater opportunities, so Keith built cars to run behind iron horses, as well as some of the first passenger cars for New York City's elevated line. Following Keith's death in 1864, his son Isaac became the company's manager, expanded the business, and moved it to Sagamore. This 1905 photograph, taken by Fred Small, shows the firm's power plant, blacksmith shop, and machine shop. The company dug the pond to supply itself with fresh water for manufacturing and for fighting neighborhood fires. The canal later came right through the pond.

19. The Keith Band was larger by far than most town bands on the cape. During the summer the Sunday evening concert was the major social event of the week. Since local newspapers did not have music critics, we have no word of how the band played, but with all that brass, it had to be loud.

20. At the center of the Nantucket Shoals is the Cross Rip Lightship, the first station of its kind in the United States, established in 1828. The vessel usually stationed at this point was built in 1865, but when this picture was taken in 1915, she was in Boston for overhaul, and her replacement was this relief vessel, which spent her years as a gypsy, moving around the coast. Besides maintaining the fixed red light and a huge foghorn, the crew of two officers and eight men operated a United States Navy radio station.

21. The most glamorous ships to sail over the shoals were the "academic twins," S.S. *Yale*, shown here, and her sister, the S.S. *Harvard*. These luxurious overnight express steamers were the Metropolitan Steamship Company's challenge to the dominance of the Fall River Line. On her maiden voyage in 1906, the *Yale* steamed the 337 miles from Boston to New York in a record fourteen hours. In 1910 the New Haven Railroad, owners of the Fall River Line, set up dummy corporations to buy and then banish the twins to the West Coast.

(*Above*)

22. The heavy work of towing coal barges to New England was done by this large tugboat fleet at Vineyard Haven. The coastal caravans, many a mile or more in length, were the marine fleets of the eastern anthracite railroads and independent barge lines. August Perry Belmont believed that once his canal was completed this lucrative traffic would pay to use it.

(*Below*)

23. Crew members of the Southeastern Massachusetts Power and Electric Company posed for their picture in Bourne in 1908. The Boston, Cape Cod and New York Canal Company used electricity to pump groundwater out of steam shovel sections during construction of the Cape Cod Canal and afterward to operate the three lift bridges and to light the canal for night traffic.

24. The Monument River, shown in this photograph dating from the early 1900s, was for centuries a winding, shallow stream with four tides per day. Joseph Jefferson, one of America's best known actors of the mid to late nineteenth century, lived across Buzzards Bay from Grover Cleveland's residence. They used to row together up the Monument River to fish. After several centuries of surveys, the last engineers came through here in 1907 for August Perry Belmont and several years later his dredges changed the river forever.

26. August Perry Belmont, builder of the Cape Cod Canal, 1853–1924.

(*Opposite*)
25. This photograph shows a New Haven Railroad passenger train pausing at the Buzzards Bay Station in 1905 before starting a run to Sandwich and "down cape" to Provincetown. The tracks entered the cape through the Village of Buzzards Bay, crossed the Monument River, and wound down the natural valley of the isthmus parallel to the route the canal would take. The branch to Falmouth turned to the left behind the water tower. This railroad was originally named the Cape Cod Central. Through a number of mergers it became part of the Old Colony Railroad, a name many Cape Codders used years after it was leased in the 1890s to J. P. Morgan's New York, New Haven and Hartford Railroad, one of many financial moves by Morgan to control transportation in New England.

27. William Barclay Parsons, the chief engineer for the Cape Cod Canal, 1859–1932.

28. The last survey before the Cape Cod Canal was built was undertaken in 1907. These two men were one of many engineering teams, working on the survey under the direction of Charles M. Thompson, of Sandwich, the resident engineer.

(Below)
29. This brief, manual effort at canal digging near Sagamore Village was personally supervised by Charles M. Thompson. One hundred laborers from Boston started swinging picks and shovels in August of 1907 in the first construction effort since Lockwood's dredge in 1884.

30. Chief Engineer Parsons, knowing that Cape Cod was formed as a terminal moraine by the last ice age, wanted to determine whether there were boulders under the surface, a common debris in such geological formations. He ordered hundreds of test borings in and around the canal route. This crew from the Western Division is drilling next to Butter- milk Bay Channel on the edge of Buzzards Bay. The borings never revealed the presence of boulders. At far right is A. S. Ackerman, head of the division, and next to him (wearing a straw hat) is Henry Welles Durham, a protégé of Parsons. Ackerman and Durham had both worked on the Panama Canal.

31. The engineering crew of the Eastern Division (seen in this photograph outside the Sandwich office of the Construction Company) was headed by Charles T. Waring, far left. The divisions were staffed by thirty men sent from the New York office. Some of them were engineers, but most were chosen because of their financial or social connections to Belmont.

32. Deeply loaded with Maine granite for the breakwater, the schooner *Annie F. Lewis* under control of the tugboat *Mary Arnold* arrived off Scusset Beach on June 19, 1909. This was the first of many shipments of stone on Maine lumber schooners—vessels that were not well suited for hauling the material. The *Annie F. Lewis* was the archetypal coastal sailer, still very much in use during the early years of the twentieth century. The oversized anchor forward on the port side was necessary to hold these ships when ground tackle was required.

(*Right*)
33. Breakwater construction moved slowly that first summer in 1909. Shallow draft work boats like this tugboat and lighter could drop stone next to the beach at high water and the evidence was visible, unlike farther out, where a broad base of granite was placed to support a pillar of stone twenty-two feet across at the top. Out in Cape Cod Bay the base is sixty-two feet wide, with enough stone to make the top of the breakwater eighteen feet above low water. The tide here has a range of 9.4 feet.

(*Above*)

34. The first piece of granite for the breakwater was on the deck of this steam lighter and ready to splash into Cape Cod Bay on June 19, 1909. The man at the right of the photograph prepares a lifting tong while signaling the winch operator to give him some slack. These men were among many blacks who worked with granite on the breakwater and for riprap along the canal banks. Blacks—usually from Baltimore, Galveston, or Beaufort, North Carolina—also worked on dredges, tugs, and scows.

(*Right*)

35. By 1913 the breakwater was completed. Most of it was made of granite from quarries at Rockport, Lanesville, and Bayview, on Cape Ann, Massachusetts.

36. The first dredge to work on Belmont's canal was the *Kennedy*, an old ladder-type machine that, although obsolete, was efficient. With her chain of buckets she started the approach channel up Buzzards Bay in August of 1909. Although she was withdrawn every winter, she worked a total of twenty-six months, during which time she removed one million cubic yards of material.

37. The hydraulic dredge *General Mac-Kenzie* was the second machine on the excavation project and the first to work the eastern end of the canal. Arriving in October, she tried to cut through the beach into the old Lockwood ditch, the first 1,500 feet of which had filled in with sand. It was a race against the bad weather of late autumn; the weather won, and the *MacKenzie* had to retreat until spring and its gentler skies.

(*Left*)
38. The cutter of the *MacKenzie* rotated at high speed, loosening material that was drawn up the main pipe by steam pumps and deposited 400-feet away through twenty-two-inch diameter pipes.

39. The fall of 1909 was a bad season for the brutal nor'easters that breed off Nova Scotia with nothing to moderate their force until they hit Cape Cod. The steam lighters and schooners working on canal construction were especially vulnerable, since the breakwater at Sandwich was not completed and there was no place of refuge nearby. One savage storm that November caught the stone fleet in Cape Cod Bay. Tugboats pulled the *General MacKenzie* to safety at Provincetown, but two lighters broke their anchor chains, swung broadside to the waves, and moved toward the beach. For the terrified crews there was nothing to do but hang on to hoisting machinery while the gale shrieked through guy wires, swung derrick booms, and pounded their ships with mountainous waves, which broke over the decks, covering them with white froth.

40. Rescuers were waiting when those tortured vessels lurched onto the beach. All sixteen men were saved; the ships broke up in the surf. There had been several such close calls before this one, and just before their ship crashed, one crewman told another, "It's time to go railroading." He did not return to the sea.

(Right)

41. Instead of waiting for the spring of 1910 to use the *Mackenzie* to open a cut through the beach at Sandwich, the contractors decided to dredge from inside the marshes to Cape Cod Bay. To do that a dredge had to be moved through Tuppers Creek and connecting streams. This land excavator and another deepened the streams through which the *Nahant*, a dredge, entered the Lockwood ditch in January of 1910.

(Below)

42. With its long boom the *Nahant* cleared the channel easily and dropped the material to either side. She reached Cape Cod Bay early in April of 1910 and then the *MacKenzie* came in through the cut.

(Right)

43. The possibility of a deep water port within the limits of the Town of Sandwich had always been a major source of enthusiasm for the canal by its citizens. They were rewarded in December of 1910 when the first cargo arrived on the coal barge *Cassie*. This vessel was somewhat of an oddity in New England waters. She was a whaleback freighter of a type introduced and used extensively on the Great Lakes. However, she was a maverick, having been built at Brooklyn, New York, and making her home port in Boston.

44. Bridge building and railroad relocation began soon after construction contracts were signed in 1909. The first phase was in the Village of Buzzards Bay, where this fleet worked on the foundations for the new rail bridge in the early fall of that year. A dredge deepens the Monument River behind the lighter unloading wooden piles onto the near bank. The wooden trestle to the right carries the single track of the Falmouth Branch.

45. After the foundations and piers were installed that winter, the bridge steel was assembled from May to September 1910.

(*Right*)
46. More than six miles of main line were relocated, most of them through the isthmus. On June 24, 1912, a New Haven passenger train hits speed on the new rails, as a safety-conscious Cape Codder chooses the abandoned track for his noonday stroll.

47. Dredges and steam shovels frequently ran into nests of glacial boulders, leaving them for the dynamiters, who reduced them with a series of blasts to chips like those in the lower foreground. This bruiser weighs about 100 tons. These prehistoric deposits delayed the canal's completion by several years.

48. The boulders the test boring never revealed were in abundance all along the route of the canal. Workmen used steam drills to shatter them for steam shovels to pick up and in some cases for powder holes to use dynamite.

49. In the Buzzards Bay Channel, dredges had an easy time with soft material until in the summer of 1911 they reached twenty-foot depths; that is where the boulders were. Divers were brought in to shatter the stone with dynamite. Using water as tamping, a charge—usually of 200 pounds—was placed, and then everyone moved back. It was noisy, slow, and expensive, but there was no other way. The kids loved it, and they gathered on the shore to wait for another thunderous roar. After a series of explosions, the dredges started up again, working until they struck something large that would not move. Then, back came the divers with their powder.

50. Some of the dredges were put out of action for awhile by boulders. The bucket of the *International* hit a boulder with this result. A few weeks of repairs and she was back to work that spring of 1913.

(Above)

51. This temporary, wooden bridge was built at Sagamore in May of 1911, primarily for workers to get to the Keith Car and Manufacturing Company. Although there were some automobiles on the cape, most people walked or used horses. Whoever arrived first by wagon got waved on by the bridge tender, who stayed in the small shed close to a stove during cold weather. The span was raised for the tugboats and scows hauling material to Cape Cod Bay for dumping.

On top of the hill in the right of the photograph is the Sagamore School.

(Below)

52. The old Sagamore Bridge, one of the two highway bridges built of the same design, was completed in the winter of 1913 and was the last bridge spanning the canal to go into service. It was two miles from the easterly entrance of the waterway. The temporary bridge is still in place and is visible in this picture with its single span raised.

53. The old Bourne Bridge was identical in design to the Sagamore Bridge, except for the former having longer approach spans and a wider roadway, thirty feet as opposed to twenty-five feet. Each bridge had a single sidewalk five feet wide with surfaces covered by oak planking. The track to the right was used by the trolley line to Monument Beach. The sign on the second pole from the right reads: "DANGER! Do not stop on the DRAW."

54. From the bridge tender's house on the north side, an operator worked the safety gates, the opening and closing of the two spans, and the signal lights to control traffic over the bridge and through the canal. The two cantilever spans could be opened or closed in about a minute. In case of a power failure, there were alternative sources: storage batteries and an emergency line to the trolley wire. On the Bourne, Sagamore, and railroad bridges the operators' houses were popular spots for nighttime poker games.

55. The dredging that began with only a few machines grew to a fleet of ten by late August of 1911, with four dredges visible in this photograph of upper Buzzards Bay taken by Fred Small from the top of the railroad bridge. The two closest machines are hydraulics, opening the mouth of the Monument River. To their left are dippers at the first turn of the Phinney's Harbor approach channel that followed the coast for nearly five miles. At far left is Gray Gables, the summer home of former Pres. Grover Cleveland. By the end of the year the channel from the rail bridge to Wings Neck was over half the charter depth at low water.

56. March 31, 1912, was launching day for the hull of the dredge *Governor Herrick*. After the hull was christened with a bottle of champagne, the vessel just sank in the sand. Local wits thought it was hilarious and typical of the way things had gone during construction.

57. The *Agnes* tried for one-half hour to pull the *Herrick* off. A week later, after three more tries, the dredge made it to the water.

58. The *Governor Warfield* at work for the first time, August 28, 1912, a few hundred feet west of the Bourne Bridge. The *Herrick* is five miles to the east and headed toward the *Warfield*. Those long steel posts opposite the middle of the scow are spuds, each seventy-feet long. Steam engines drove them into the bottom, and like stilts they raised the *Warfield* several feet to keep her stationary. The fifty-seven-foot boom allowed dredging to a depth of forty-feet, an extraordinary capability. Each vessel had two crews of a dozen men each. They worked for twelve hours, rested for twelve. They had two days off per year: Christmas and July Fourth.

59. The steam drills made a fearsome noise, but despite that the pup in the foreground could not resist the opportunity to see what was going on.

60. The crewmen of the *Warfield* are inside the dredge and the men with drills sought shelter elsewhere when dynamite charges demolished boulders. The big rocks near the Bourne Bridge were on the surface and easily removed. This photograph and the preceding one were both taken on May 3, 1913.

(Below)
61. With the early construction of the canal going slowly, August Perry Belmont urged the contractors to bring in more equipment. Late in the fall of 1910, the *Capitol* and two dredges of similar design were bought from a bankrupt New York company. The three worked until the canal opened in 1914. Though sturdy and reliable, they had but one-third or less the capacity of the *Warfield* or *Herrick*. In all, twenty-six dredges had to be used.

62. The *National,* one of the obsolete dipper dredges, developed a serious leak in her hull in May of 1914. This was not uncommon among older wooden vessels, most of which were so limber they needed constant pumping to stay afloat. Even auxiliary pumps could not prevent the inevitable, so the engine room crew dumped her fires to prevent a boiler explosion. Some of the crewmen went ashore on a skiff; the others swam. Later, divers patched her hull and refloated the *National* to work again. Across the water are the White Cliffs in Bourne on the south bank of the canal.

63. In January of 1914 steam shovels and dredges were close together in Bournedale and the canal's opening was only seven months away. The natural dam carrying the track across the trench to the right was at Station No. 216. As first planned that was the farthest east that steam shovels would dig. When dredges were slowed by boulders, the contractors decided to use shovels for another 800 feet to Station No. 208, the barrier at the far end of the trench. Steam shovels proved to be the most efficient way to dig, since each of them averaged 23,000 cubic yards per month. They dug 7,000 feet of canal, and if the contractors had used them sooner—as suggested by Chief Engineer Parsons—the job could have been finished two years earlier. Pumps at the center right drain the trench. In the background, throwing clouds of steam is the *Governor Herrick*.

64. The Reuben Collins family ran a farm at this site in Bournedale for several generations until all these heavy smokers showed up in 1913. Steam shovels, unlike dredges, worked in the daylight hours. The nights were quiet except for a hostler moving around the trench, stoking fires and maintaining steam for the crews who left their bunks in nearby box cars at first light in the morning sky.

(*Below*)
65. The Collins farmhouse, at the left of the photograph, lost some of its foundation when railroad tracks were laid past the front door. Later the house was moved farther back. This photograph was taken for a popular magazine, *Frank Leslie's Weekly*.

66. At this point in Bournedale, the
north bank is nearly cleaned out and
these shovels will be moved west. A series
of natural dams was left in place to
divide the trench into sections to hold
back ocean water at the headings. Cutting through one dam at a time allowed
dredging to be done gradually rather
than all at once, with a "closing of the
Red Sea" effect.

(*Right*)
67. Each section had a ditch to allow
groundwater to run toward a pumping
station like the one at Station No. 276,
the farthest west that steam shovels
worked. The building to the left in the
photograph had four electric pumps and
one steam pump, which proved more
than enough to keep the trench dry.

68. By May of 1913 most of the land cut was under construction, so Parsons invited Belmont and the major investors to see the progress. They arrived in early June on Belmont's private railroad car at the Village of Buzzards Bay. After sailing under the two new bridges the party came to this inland lake the dredge *Federal* was enlarging. To accommodate his important guests, Parsons, standing at the right, had four rows of benches built on this scow, giving it the appearance of a floating church. Belmont is seated in the front row on the far side, next to his wife, an avid amateur photographer who kept taking pictures for her scrapbook.

69. An hour later the inspection party
was in a Bournedale steam shovel section, where it was sooty and rough,
riding behind a narrow gauge locomotive over temporary track through the
trench. But despite the discomfort,
August Perry Belmont was a happy man;
the dream of centuries—a canal across
Cape Cod—was coming true. And he had
made it so.

70. This photograph shows August Perry Belmont blending the waters of Cape Cod and Buzzards Bay, on April 21, 1914, while prophesying the happiness and prosperity his new waterway would bring.

71. Following the blending of the waters, the small earthen dam in the lower part of the photograph was demolished by hand shoveling, including a couple of swings by Belmont. The waters from Cape Cod Bay ran between Belmont, on the left, extending his hand, and Parsons, reaching for a handshake. At the far left is Edward Foley, the steam shovel contractor. Above Foley, wearing a derby, is Comdr. Jacob W. Miller, first vice president and general manager of the Cape Cod Construction Company.

(*Right*)
72. Then Belmont, Foley, and the others examine the flume from the opposite side. Belmont returned that day to New York after announcing the dyke would be removed July Fourth, an idea that did not please the contractors.

73. It is June 9, 1914, and the Boston excursion steamer, *Dorothy Bradford*, is arriving in Sandwich, the first passenger ship to do so. Most of those aboard are civil engineers, faculty members, and students from the Massachusetts Institute of Technology—with a professional interest in the huge construction project. A few of the many craft in the working fleet are visible, including a tugboat pulling an empty scow back to the heading in Bournedale after a trip to dump material far out in Cape Cod Bay.

74. Current passing through Foley's
Dyke, July 4, 1914.

75. Effect of current.

76. For the first time the sister dredges built at opposite ends of the canal appear in the same photograph. The *Governor Warfield*, at the right, seems to be the object of attention for the Cape Codder who has stopped his team of horses on the road the Canal Company built along the north bank. The *Governor Herrick* still has to remove the remains of Foley's Dyke. It is July 7, 1914.

Mr. August Belmont, President
and the Directors of the
Cape Cod Construction Company
request the pleasure of your company
at the opening of the
Cape Cod Canal
on Wednesday, the twenty-ninth of July
Nineteen hundred and fourteen

R.S.V.P.
Forty-three Exchange Place
New York

78. Belmont sent formal invitations to attend the canal's opening to local, state, and national political figures and to his closest friends in finance, industry, and transportation.

(*Opposite*)

77. The water raced through this shallow area of the canal with such velocity that the *Governor Herrick* broke both her stern spuds while dredging. The *Governor Warfield* stayed healthy and so got the assignment to remove the rest of Foley's Dyke. Within two weeks the channel was fifteen feet deep and these rapids disappeared. In those final days in July of 1914 things were hectic and everyone was under pressure, for it was almost time to open the Cape Cod Canal.

79. To attract business Belmont had advertisements placed on the marine pages of newspapers in cities where traffic originated. This ad appeared in the *Boston Globe*, Thursday, July 23, 1914. But from July 26, Europe's mobilization for World War I dominated the front pages, and the great amount of publicity the company hoped for never materialized. The *New York Times* story on the canal's opening was on page 6.

80. Belmont had gold and silver medals, nearly two inches in diameter, minted for those he felt had made major contributions to the canal. The gold went to Parsons, contractors, major investors, and himself. This is the front of such a medal; the obverse was lettered: "First Traffic Across The Isthmus/September 2, 1627/Official Opening of Canal July 29, 1914."

81. Belmont chartered the S.S. *Rose Standish*, the newest vessel in the Boston Harbor excursion fleet, to officially open the canal on Wednesday, July 29, 1914. She was the first passenger ship to transit the waterway, passing west on her way to New Bedford the day before. Here she is leading the Parade of Ships opening day and steaming east. It is almost 1:30 P.M. and she's a few hundred feet away from cutting a ribbon strung across the canal. Cape Codders had never seen anything like it! Not only did they finally have their canal, but a lot more—if only temporarily: visitors, town bands, ships, fireworks, dances, parades, decorations on stores and homes and even August Perry Belmont's private railroad car, across the water at the end of that train.

82. Belmont brought more than his railroad car. This sleek yacht, the *Scout*, belonged to him, too. It was the third ship in that nautical parade that officially opened the canal. The *Scout* sailed through without the owner aboard, as he had stayed on the *Rose Standish* from New Bedford, where his guests had arrived that morning by train from New York, Boston, and Newport.

83. There were other millionaires' yachts, including the *Sultana*, a 187-foot chunk of luxury living owned by Mrs. E. H. Harriman, daughter-in-law of the builder of the Union Pacific Railroad. *Sultana* is just west of the railroad bridge. The two steam lighters are tied to dolphins, or pile clusters, used to mark the channel and for mooring. That is Gray Gables to the left.

84. Farther east in Bournedale, Fred Small's camera captures *Sultana* sailing through the canal "at lowest speed that will afford steerageway," according to the company's rules for passage. When Small could not find a convenient hill from which to film, he climbed bridges, water towers and houses to record a story that took place in his front yard.

85. Belmont, the canal builder, with hands folded and Massachusetts Gov. David I. Walsh were at Sandwich for the simultaneous 275th anniversary of the town and the opening of the waterway. Sandwich citizens gave Belmont a loving cup, and he told them that since his mother had come from there, "If you wish to claim me on that score, we can enter upon your town records . . . the Cape Cod Canal had its origin in Sandwich."

(Below)
86. Belmont spoke from this platform at Town Neck, where an estimated five thousand people gathered that afternoon, following a parade of fifty floats. Governor Walsh, shown here, congratulated Sandwich on its anniversary, said the canal was of great importance to the commercial interests of Boston and all New England, and paid tribute to Belmont for his spirit and energy.

87. The other vessels in the Parade of Ships were strangers to the canal, but this pair, the *Sarah*, left, and the *Agnes*, had been around as working craft since construction began. The buildings across the water seen above the tugboats are part of the Keith Car and Manufacturing Company.

(*Opposite*)
88. This map shows the appearance of the Cape Cod Canal as it was from its opening in 1914 until its expansion in the 1930s.

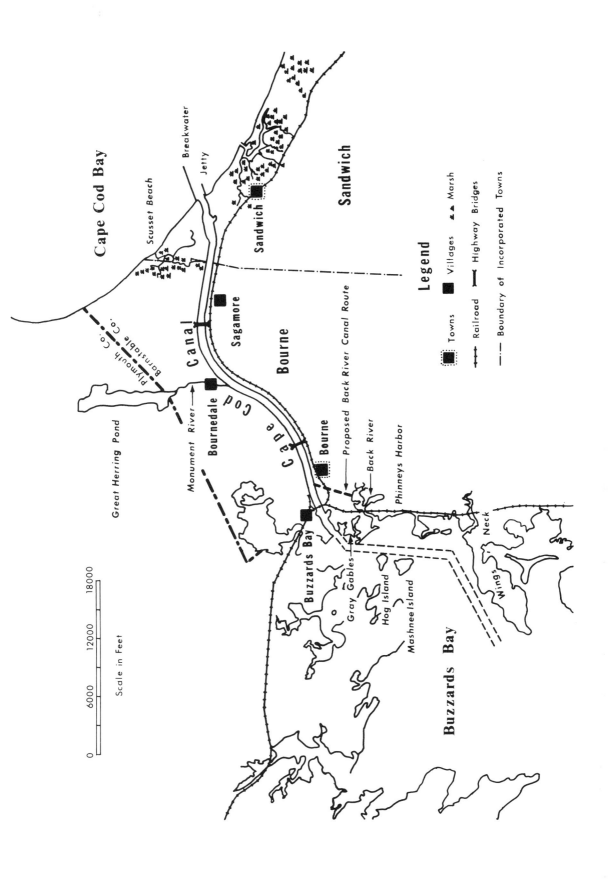

89. One of the finest panoramic photographs of the early days of the canal was taken from a bluff during the first week of August of 1914. The Bournedale Railroad Station is seen on the south bank of the canal in back of the wooden, docklike structure that is all that remains of the temporary bridge first built in Sagamore and then moved here after the permanent steel lift bridge was opened for traffic. Some years later a ferry operated across the canal at this point. The long "S" curve of the canal to the west is visible, except for a few trees in the distance. The granite riprap is neatly piled along the lower banks through this section to prevent erosion from ships' wakes. The wooden fence between the two houses marks the edge of the road along the north side of the canal.

90. Another celebration, the pageant of Cape Cod, was held for four days in the middle of August of 1914. Various historical moments of the Cape Cod story were dramatized, using costumes of the depicted era. This is the field on the south bank of the canal adjacent to the Bourne Bridge with the old and the new in proximity—trolley cars, automobiles, the canal, and recreated history. Official delegations were sent to the pageant from most towns on the cape. Admission to the event was free; the program cost ten cents.

91. With a controlling depth (point of least water) of only fifteen feet, mariners did not line up to use the canal after its opening. The tugboat *Albert J. Stone* hauling three empty schooner-barges following a coal trip to northern New England was the canal's first real commercial business. This Erie Railroad tow sailed west on August 12, 1914. The president of the Erie Railroad was a director of the Canal Company, and he ordered his marine fleet to use the waterway.

92. Belmont's traffic surveys showed that of the 25 million tons of cargo carried annually through Nantucket Sound, 9 million tons was coal. He believed coal transport would provide the largest source of the canal's income. When the waterway opened the shallow channel could not accommodate loaded vessels of any size, so tows continued to use the outside route when loaded, with some of them returning empty via the canal, like the Lehigh and Wilkes Barre Coal Company's tugboat *Honeybrook* with three schooner-barges. These ships carried Pennsylvania anthracite from New York Harbor coal docks to Boston, Portland, and ports farther north, where the Maine Central Railroad delivered it inland.

93. Often a tow could not transit the
canal easily. If the current was running
against it, the tow would be broken up
at the entrance with the tugboat pulling
one barge through at a time, a process
often requiring five trips. This caused
delays, as did the one-way traffic. These
tugboats had two crews for continuous
operations, for the economy in towing
was in the steady movement of ships.
Since tolls added to costs the canal was
an advantage to shippers only if there
were no delays. The Canal Company
could not guarantee that. The huge tugboat *Perth Amboy* of the Lehigh Valley
Railroad came through about once per
week from 1916 until after World War
II. On July 21, 1918, the *Perth Amboy*
was badly damaged by shells from a German submarine off Chatham. The next
day the United States government took
over the canal.

94. This photograph shows three potential customers that did not use the canal. These schooner-barges of the Reading Railroad were cut loose from the tugboat *Mars* off Truro during a savage storm on April 4, 1915. The crew of the *Mars* cut the hawser to save themselves. Each of these 200-foot-long vessels carried a crew of four, and despite their sails they were not designed to move independently as wind ships. Under the circumstances all their crews could do was stay with their ships, riding the breakers onto the Great Beach, where they were helped to safety by the United States Life Saving Service from Highland Station, just back of the bluff to the left.

From foreground to background these barges are the *Coleraine, Manheim,* and *Tunnel Ridge.* Only the *Manheim* was salvaged to sail again; the other two had their bottoms torn out.

95. One of the great American luxury yachts, heading west in July of 1915, Cornelius Vanderbilt's *North Star* was 256 feet long, making her larger than many commercial steamers of her time. Her nine magnificent staterooms with paneled walls, parquet floors, oriental rugs, and custom-built furniture provided the Vanderbilt family an opulent milieu for shorter voyages between New York City and their summer estate at Newport and longer cruises across the Atlantic to their other homes abroad. The *North Star* had a large dining room furnished entirely in the style known as Louis XIV; the library had a handsome, fake fireplace built in accordance with the owner's wishes to duplicate the comforts of his life ashore. The ship's radio was handy in passing on business decisions to executives who had not the time for marine wanderings, and the radio operator was constantly on duty during those hours the New York Stock Exchange was open. A courier would stand by ready to bring Vanderbilt word on quotations in which he had expressed an interest. The *North Star* cost $250,000. Its upkeep was something else; Vanderbilt did not discuss it.

96. Barges and schooners of shallow draft used the canal from its opening. They always went through under tow, as the company would not permit vessels without power to transit without a tug. Lumber from Down East and Canada, lime from Rockland, Maine, and plaster from Nova Scotia went west in great quantities. Later granite from Cape Ann, Massachusetts, and from Maine for use in breakwaters, roads, and buildings was a frequent cargo.

97. A hydraulic dredge deepens the channel just west of the railroad bridge as a "T-Wharf" tug, the *Zetes*, tows a barge, the *Elizabeth*, a vessel obviously designed for canals far narrower than Belmont's new waterway. The *Elizabeth* may have come east from the Great Lakes, possibly taking on a load of flour at Buffalo and reaching here via the Erie Canal, the Hudson River, and Long Island Sound.

98. In order to provide twenty-four hour service for shipping, the canal was lighted at night. There were 154 lights like this on poles, placed in pairs, at or near the high water mark every 500 feet for the length of the canal in the land cut. Every Saturday morning the lights were turned on and an electrician was taken by a boatman with a small craft to each of these poles, replacing the burned out bulbs. Today mercury vapor lamps are used.

99. Chief Engineer Parsons still had to contend with his old nemesis: boulders. They were found in great numbers, often by divers. Removing them was a slow process, since diving could only be done at slack water. Sometimes divers placed slings around the boulders for removal by steam lighters. A final count in 1916 showed about 700 boulders weighing in all some 3,500 tons were removed by divers using slings or explosives.

100. Steam colliers were widely used along the East Coast after 1907, and many of them became regular canal customers after the channel was dredged to twenty-five feet. The *Cicoa*, tied to dolphins in Buzzards Bay, is similar in design to Great Lakes ore boats. She is just off the fairway in Phinneys Harbor Channel, probably awaiting clearance on this cold winter day.

101. In warmer weather, excursion steamers were frequently seen in the canal. A local company, calling itself the Cape Cod Canal Route, ran daily excursions charging one dollar for a round trip. Larger vessels from Boston and New Bedford appeared on summer weekends.

102. This photograph of the Eastern Steamship Lines' *Old Colony* on her trial run through the canal was taken by Fred Small. Small set up his camera and tripod on the north bank near Station No. 235 where Foley's Dyke was cut through on July 4, 1914.

103. The *Massachusetts*, seen in this photograph approaching Pier 19 in New York Harbor, made frequent transits through the Cape Cod Canal in 1916 and 1917. In addition to providing income for the canal, these runs ensured the Canal Company excellent publicity through Eastern's advertising of the service. The *Massachusetts* was later sunk during the Japanese raid on Pearl Harbor, but was raised and reconditioned for the duration of World War II.

(*Below*)
104. The *Bunker Hill*, sister ship to the *Massachusetts*, is seen here in the Cape Cod Canal. She later served in World War II as an aircraft tender and then was used as a gambling ship off the coast of Long Beach, California—a career cut short by a Coast Guard raid.

(*Left*)

105. It has long been a practice in merchant marine training to teach cadets to run sailing vessels. This is one of the better known ships in that class, the *Newport*, of the New York State Merchant Marine Academy, on her annual summer cruise in 1916. She is underway on auxiliary power.

(*Right*)

106. During World War I, Keith Car and Manufacturing Company at Sagamore built hundreds of boxcars like this "Forty and Eight" for the American Expeditionary Force in France. The name was derived from their capacity: they held forty men or eight horses.

(*Below*)

107. United States Navy submarines used the Cape Cod Canal, beginning in World War I. Most of them, like the U.S.S. *1*, sailing west on February 27, 1919 were assigned to the big naval facility at New London, Connecticut. At that time government vessels paid six cents per gross ton toll, with a minimum charge of eight dollars.

108. Two popular steamers that used the canal were the *North Star* and the *Calvin Austin*. Built in 1901 for Eastern Steamship Lines' Boston-Yarmouth run, the *North Star* was used occasionally for New York-Boston Metropolitan Line service, as in this 1918 photograph taken in Bournedale. The *North Star* also served on the New York-Portland run that took twenty-five hours via Nantucket Sound but only eighteen hours once the canal opened.

109. The *Calvin Austin*, a comfortable, seaworthy vessel, was built in 1903 for Eastern's International Line from Boston to New Brunswick. She was named after an Eastern executive who became the line's president after its founder, Charles W. Morse, was sent to Atlanta Penitentiary. The *Calvin Austin* was used on the New York-Boston run for summer service from 1920 to 1923 and occasionally served on other Eastern lines, when traffic warranted. Though the *Calvin Austin* and the *North Star* were primarily passenger steamers, both these ships carried freight—most of it high quality merchanise for next-day delivery. To New England manufacturers, these overnight boats were an asset in handling their priority freight, since rail delivery took four or five days.

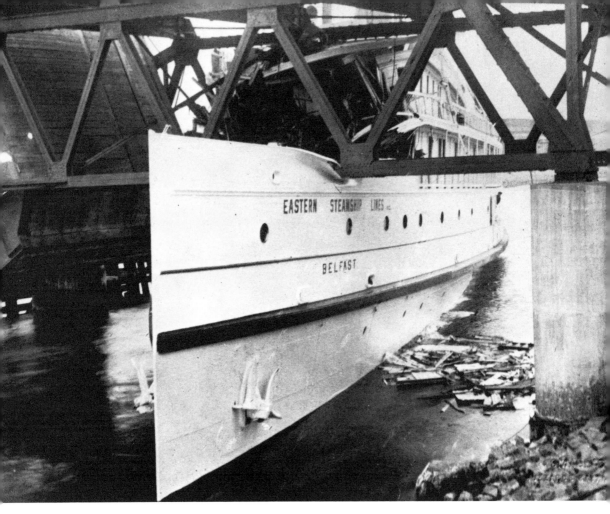

110. On April 16, 1919, on her first trip of the season, the *Belfast*, of the Eastern Steamship Lines, was caught in a stiff breeze and a cross-current—the worst combination for mariners—in the Cape Cod Canal. As a result of the ship's collision with the Sagamore Bridge, an officer and two passengers were injured in the pilot house and the forward super-structure. With her stern in mid-channel and her bow snuggled under the north span of the bridge, as if to keep warm, the *Belfast* blocked the canal for thirty hours; road traffic was detoured over Bourne Bridge.

111. This photograph, taken on April 16 from the south bank of the canal, shows the *Belfast* still stuck under the Sagamore Bridge with a tugboat standing by to bring the steamship to a ship-yard in Boston. The trip was made on April 17. The repairs of the *Belfast* took two weeks and cost $10,000. Sagamore Bridge was not damaged.

(Above)

112. Cape winters were cold in the 1920s with heavy snow on occasion. A trio of canal employees posed for this photograph taken by Fred Small in 1925 at the Buzzards Bay Railroad Station.

(Left)

113. Cape Codders could get on a train at the Buzzards Bay Station and change at New York for the Florida-bound "Everglades," a luxury train with parlor car, or they could stay and freeze. Most people stayed and used bed comforters to warm their automobiles, as can be seen on Main Street at the left. The canal is about five hundred feet beyond the railroad cars. Next to the curb is the trolley line to Monument Beach. Fred Small's shop is in the middle of that row of stores.

(Right)

114. By 1932, the business district of the village had expanded, since Buzzards Bay was the western gateway to the cape and more Americans had automobiles and were traveling farther for vacations. During the summer months motorists often had a long wait for the canal's drawbridges to close, since the good weather brought out yachtsmen in great numbers.

115. Ship watching became a popular evening activity when passenger steamers started using the canal in 1916, and it reached new heights of attendance in June of 1924 with the arrival of the brand new sister ships *Boston* and *New York* of the Eastern Steamship Lines. It was the evening, or "New York boat," that drew the crowds. Against the current the trip took about an hour. In this photograph the *Boston* is in Bournedale at the narrowest part of the canal, called "the eye of the needle" by local residents. In good weather people would gather on the slopes by the canal, among the trees, and close to the water. The highway bridges were good vantage points, and those who lived near the Bourne Bridge often arrived early to stop for a cone at an ice cream parlor, The Three Mile Look, on the north bank, and then stroll out to the water to wait. Usually it was a youngster who first shouted, "There she is!"

116 and 117. The white twins, the *Boston* (left) and the *New York* (below), were successful from their maiden voyages and they became symbols of the canal. Each had cost nearly $2 million and their size —402-feet long, seventy-two-feet wide, and 5,000 tons weight—made them comfortable to ride. With a capacity of 900 passengers and cargo space for 700 tons each, they set records for passengers carried and profits earned. Eastern Steam-

ship Lines touted the canal as the highlight of the voyage, so most passengers were on deck for the transit, as on the *Boston*. Early and late in the season the sight was spectacular, with all the lights on, the orchestra playing, the ship's searchlight sweeping the shores, and the captain sending greetings on her whistle. The morning transit, or "Boston boat," never drew shore crowds, but many passengers were on deck at 5:00 A.M.

(*Below*)
118. In April of 1928 the *New York* ran aground early one morning near Saga-

more Bridge. She was not damaged and was refloated on the next tide; tugboats and motorboats removed the passengers.

119. Ever since the spring of 1916, Eastern's ships had used the canal. In the fall of 1927, citing "persistent public demand," the New York-Boston service was in operation daily throughout the year, as the line had the steamers to do it. Eastern had been acquiring control of the Old Dominion Line, an established New York-Norfolk company that had two open ocean boats delivered in 1924. The *George Washington*, shown here, and her sister, the *Robert E. Lee*, were 390 feet long and weighed 5,184 tons each. On March 10, 1928, the *Lee* strayed inside her course and went aground on rocks south of Plymouth. The Coast Guard from the Manomet Point Station rescued all 263 people aboard the following morning. After the rescue a surf boat capsized, drowning three coastguardsmen. The *Lee* was repaired.

EASTERN
STEAMSHIP LINES
Eleven Coastwise Services

BOSTON ✦ NEW YORK
BOSTON ✦ BANGOR
BOSTON ✦ PORTLAND
BOSTON ✦ ST·JOHN·*NB*
BOSTON & YARMOUTH STEAMSHIP COMPANY

BAR HARBOR LINE   BLUE HILL LINE

EFFECTIVE NOVEMBER 12, 1928
REVISED TO JANUARY 2, 1929

(Left)
120. The Eastern Steamships Lines timetable cover showed a summer boat on one side and a winter boat on the other.

121. Effective November 12, 1928, a one-way ticket on Eastern Steamship Lines' Boston-New York run cost five dollars, not including a stateroom or meals.

122. Ship's passengers going through the canal enjoyed watching the bridge spans open ahead of their vessel and close after them. This is the Sagamore Bridge taken from the Nantasket Beach Steamboat Company's *Norumbega*, heading west on May 28, 1933.

123 and 124. The *Norumbega* was built in 1902 at Bath, Maine, for the Maine Central's Mt. Desert ferry run and was brought to Massachusetts in 1930; she made frequent trips through the Cape Cod Canal, stopping at the State Pier, and at the Village of Buzzards Bay (*above*) before heading back to Boston (*left*).

125. Steam gave way to diesel power after World War II (*below*), but excursions continued on the *Boston Belle*.

126. This is a rare, aerial photograph of the Cape Cod Canal, taken from a plane over Buzzards Bay in 1931, before the canal was widened. For the first few years under government ownership the canal remained unchanged: it was narrow and winding. The New Haven Railroad Bridge at Buzzards Bay is in the lower foreground. The original Bourne Bridge is in the center of the photograph. A freighter is seen having cleared Bourne Bridge and heading east. Shoals on both sides of the channel are clearly visible in the foreground. The Army Corps of Engineers was working on plans to make it a much larger waterway.

127. Work began on the substructures of both new highway bridges on December 8, 1933, and were completed on May 1, 1934, when steel starting going up for the superstructures. In July of 1934 Fred Small took this photograph of the Bourne Bridge on the south bank.

(Opposite)

128. Both phases of the bridge improvement program are shown in this picture of the Bourne Bridge, taken on August 10, 1934. Bridge steel is at mid-point from the south bank, while the *Governor Herrick* on the opposite side of the channel—twenty-two years after she took her first dipperful of sand from the canal—is widening the work she helped to create.

(Above)

129. By the summer of 1935 the new channel was 205 feet wide and both the new Bourne Bridge, at the top of the photograph, and the new Sagamore Bridge had been in use since June 21. The extremes of the waterway are indicated by the riprapped banks to either side.

(Right)

130. To carry trains across the wider canal, the world's largest single-span life bridge at that time was built at the Village of Buzzards Bay. The 2,050-ton span is lowered and raised by electric motors and a 1,000-ton counterweight at the base of each tower.

131. Additional federal appropriations paid for further widening of the canal. In the summer of 1936, cranes dug "in the dry," while the *Governor Herrick* deepened the channel. The new south bank was complete and covered with heavier riprap.

132. Farther east, at Sagamore, construction was interrupted on January 27, 1937 when the *Herrick* suddenly sank. Fortunately, she was outside the channel and ships could pass her. The old road along the north bank of the canal has seen its traffic move to the new highway at the left. Sagamore Bridge is in the background.

133. The sidewheeler *Priscilla*—one of four steamers of America's most famous overnight service, the Fall River Line— was the only passenger ship of that company to use the Cape Cod Canal. Due to a New York shipyard strike, she was ordered to Boston for repairs in drydock. *Priscilla* sailed east on June 17, 1937, returning two days later. She had a beam of ninety-three feet and was the widest ship to transit the canal up to that time. Eastern's ships had drained off great numbers of passengers and their year-round service, beginning in the late fall of 1927 had made the end of the Fall River Line a certainty. A month after this photograph was taken, the Fall River Line foundered in a court room when a federal judge granted the owners, the New Haven Railroad, permission to end the ninety-year-old service and sell the four steamers for scrap.

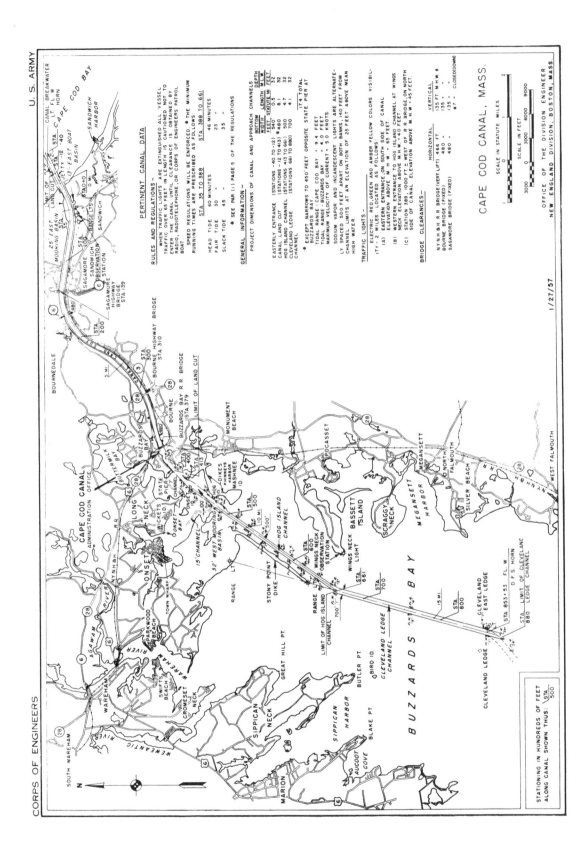

134. Map of the present Cape Cod Canal.

135. Submarines and their attendant vessels were common sights in the canal before the age of nuclear propulsion. The U.S.S. *Falcon*, a rescue ship with her diving bell at the stern, may be heading to the United States Navy Base at New London, in this photograph taken on April 17, 1940.

136. The S.S. *Sandcraft*, a hopper dredge, cruises over shoal spots to pick up sand with suction pipes below her bridge. That pipe work kept the channel of the canal thirty-two feet deep. The Army Corps of Engineers has several newer vessels of similar design, which visit the canal once per year to dredge.

137. The United Fruit Company's S.S. *Abangarez*, one of the smaller banana steamers that sailed between Central America and East Coast ports, is shown at Sandwich, on November 5, 1940, westbound and a few hours out of Boston. United Fruit called its ships the Great White Fleet.

138. From 1916 until World War II small coastal freighters were a common sight in the canal, lumbering along on their single, reciprocating engines. Eastern's S.S. *Sandwich* was typical of that class, which had the same general appearance as tramp steamers. These simple, reliable ships earned their keep and Eastern had a small fleet of them. In the early 1930s, eleven were engaged in year-round transportation from Norfolk to Yarmouth, Nova Scotia.

139. One of the oldest passenger steamers in service on the East Coast was the S.S. *Juniata* passing Sandwich Control Station on October 2, 1940. Built at Wilmington, Delaware, in 1897, *Juniata* was a frequent visitor in ports from Boston, to which she is heading, to as far south as Miami, the southern terminus of her owners, the Merchants and Miners Line, an old Baltimore concern. That company had a steamer sailing from Miami to Boston every Wednesday and from Baltimore every Tuesday. One way fare from Miami to Boston was $49.00. Round trip was $80.00. Both tickets included meals and a berth. The better staterooms cost from $2.25 to $32.00 in addition; the latter were luxurious. You could bring along your automobile for another $35.00.

140. Most accidents in the canal have not been serious—but some have. On January 27, 1938, the collier *Everett* rammed the tugboat *Plymouth*, putting the smaller craft on the bottom in three minutes. Benjamin S. Harrison was on traffic control duty at Sandwich, that building with a tower across the water in the photograph. Harrison took off in a launch and rescued eleven men from the cold water; the Coast Guard picked up four. One man was lost. A diver is examining the wreck, later removed by dynamite.

(*Left*)

141. On June 28, 1942, the collier *Stephen R. Jones*, out of Norfolk for Boston with coal, hit the north bank of the canal near Bourne Bridge and sank, closing the waterway. On July 4, a salvage firm exploded the first of a series of dynamite charges in her hull. On the last day of the month the final blast spread what was left of the *Jones* around the bottom.

142. The freighter *Arizona Sword* sank May 5, 1951, after a collision with a collier. She lay on the bottom for over a year next to the north bank in Sandwich before she was salvaged and her cargo of sulphur recovered.

143. Early during World War II the United States Navy quickly put deck guns on just about everything afloat, including the old steam collier, *Jason*, which is seen here westbound and without cargo, passing the Sandwich Control Station on January 31, 1942.

(*Left*)

144. Not long after that one of the strangest ships to transit the canal during the war came through, heading east, on the chilly morning of February 14, 1942. She is the Russian ice breaker *Krassin*. What this ancient coal burner was doing so far from home is lost to us. The canal records merely indicate her passage.

(*Below*)

145. On the blustery afternoon of March 27, 1942, a former British cruise liner, the *Queen of Bermuda*, arrived under tow for a New York shipyard. It had been a long, slow trip for the former Furness Lines vessel, which had sheared a propeller off Nova Scotia. The two tugs with white hulls are "T" Wharf Company ships from Boston. The others are Canadian salvage vessels. Several days later, the *Queen of Bermuda* was drydocked at New York, fitted with a new prop, and returned to service as a troop ship.

146. A United States Navy blimp, the *K-3*, patrols the canal above Sandwich on June 10, 1942, before the arrival of a convoy of merchant ships from the Buzzards Bay assembly area. These airships flew from their base at South Weymouth, just below Quincy, and were a frequent sight around the canal. Although they had a maximum speed of sixty-five knots, blimps usually cruised at about fifty knots. They could stay in the air for long periods of time and were equipped with radar to find submarines and with depth charges and machine guns to attack them.

(*Above*)

147. The years of World War II saw many damaged ships sail through the canal on their way to New York shipyards, like this torpedo victim moving west past Buzzards Bay Traffic Control. She was luckier than most, since—despite having her bow shot out—she is afloat and under her own power.

148. Many damaged ships had to be towed, as the British tanker *G. S. Walden* did on September 28, 1942, by "T" Wharf tugboats from Boston. The *Walden* had been in a convoy from Halifax to Britain when a torpedo under her stern blew away her propellers and rudder. That first year America was in the war, German submarines sank over two million tons of United States shipping along the East Coast and convoy routes to Europe. In the awful spring and summer of 1942, merchant seamen called the North Atlantic "torpedo alley."

149. One had to look closely at some ships during the war to identify them. On September 3, 1942, both the *Boston* and the *New York* sailed east as members of a British convoy, assembling at Halifax. The twins had been sold to Britain under Lend-Lease. The other vessels in the parade that day were also coastal passenger steamers, a fleet identified by their British volunteer crews as "the honeymoon convoy." Just twenty-two days later, H.M.S. *Boston* and H.M.S. *New York* were torpedoed in the North Atlantic and sank.

150. The British liner *Franconia*, at peace (*above*) and war (*below*), sailing through Buzzards Bay.

151, 152, and 153. The Cape Cod Canal during three days in May of 1942 looked like this, with a variety of merchantmen headed for war. The *Myrmidon* (151) and the *Empire Snow* (152) are British, the *Santa Elisa* (153) is a United States Army cargo vessel. The *Myrmidon* will be convoyed up the coast to Halifax—then to Murmansk, Russia. The *Empire Snow* and the *Santa Elisa* will pick up escorts off Provincetown and sail to Casco Bay, Maine, to wait for a larger convoy to form before sailing for Britain. Cana-

dian and American destroyers and corvettes did most of the convoy duty, and at first there were never enough of them. In May of 1942 the Nazi submarine fleet in the western Atlantic numbered thirty-five, by June it was forty, with twenty more vessels launched per month. The American navy was so short of anti-submarine vessels that U-boats were surfacing within sight of the coast and sinking merchant ships with gunfire, saving torpedoes for the bigger targets at night.

The destruction was ruthless and widespread. The *Myrmidon* has her life boats swung out in case of attack and the urgent need to lower them quickly. The *Santa Elisa* and the *Empire Snow* have military vehicles stacked on deck, a common practice. That bowspritlike device on the *Empire Snow* was used to trail paravanes to cut cables on submerged mines, a Nazi weapon planted in shallow waters around Britain by planes and submarines.

154. The building of the Cape Cod Canal divided the isthmus. Keith Car and Manufacturing Company was on the south side of the waterway, while most of its employees lived on the north side. The business district of Buzzards Bay that also served Bourne was on the north side. Most of the customers lived on the south side. The churches were all on the south side, but many of the parishioners lived on the north side. Getting to church by the bridge was a four-mile drive—or walk. The Episcopalians started their own church in the Village of Buzzards Bay in 1938, using a local lodge. Nine years later they had raised enough money to buy an unused church in Hull, Massachusetts, sixty miles up the coast. Moving it over highways would have been far too costly, so it was loaded on this barge and brought by water. The trip was eventful: foul weather forced the tug to seek shelter for several days, and a broken towing cable almost lost the church in Cape Cod Bay. On a spring day in 1947, Benjamin S. Harrison was in a plane when he took this photograph of the only church to sail the Cape Cod Canal. At slack water it was rolled over the bank and several months later moved to its Main Street location. The church is called Saint Peter's-on-the-Canal, after the biblical Big Fisherman.

155. Large, vertical windows offer excellent visibility to the Marine Traffic Controllers who have a ringside view from their headquarters in the Village of Buzzards Bay of the ships that pass through the Cape Cod Canal each year, including the excursion ship *New Shoreham*, heading west.

156. Traffic control on the western end of the canal used to operate from Wings Neck. Now television cameras and radar send what they see to Buzzards Bay. A television camera and radar share the platform at the top of the tower at the right. A second camera is mounted next to the ladder above the half-way point. Their signals reach the traffic control office via the microwave relay cone just below the platform. Each television camera is independent and remote controlled.

157. Centralized ship traffic control is accomplished with the latest electronic devices at the Cape Cod Canal. Here William D. Donovan of Sandwich answers a call from a ship on the VHF radio telephone.

158. The patrol boat *Renier* has daily chores at the canal—enforcing regulations, performing rescue operations, boating safety, and hydrographic surveys in shallow waters. The *Renier* is a steel-hulled forty-five footer with twin diesels. She is just loafing along here, posing for her picture.

159. The East Boat Basin is off the south bank at Sandwich. It has over eight acres of water; the outer half is dredged to thirteen feet at low water, the inner half to eight feet. On the western end there is a dredged channel northwest from Hog Island Channel to Onset Bay. These boat basins are necessary places of refuge, supplies, and anchorage. Mooring basins for large ships are at either end of the canal, too.

160. Buzzards Bay photographer Benjamin S. Harrison spotted the collier *Consolidation Coal* sailing west past the clipped end of Hog Island one clear afternoon in the 1950s. She is empty and riding high, creating a huge bow wave and a boiling wake. The second island, to the upper right of the photograph, is Mashnee. The Army Corps of Engineers created the new channel and connected the two islands and the cape with a causeway to prevent silting in the new channel from the old, which took a turn off Gray Gables and followed the coast to the left of Hog Island.

161. With much of its cargo topside, this French container ship is typical of a common class of freighters in North Atlantic service today.

162. The glamor ships only come back now and again to the canal. This big, white two-stacker is the *Kungsholm*, of the Swedish-American Line, heading for New York on the last leg of a North Atlantic crossing. The steamer at the left, broadside, is the S.S. *Bay State*, training ship of the Massachusetts Maritime Academy, berthed at the State Pier at the western edge of the campus in the Village of Buzzards Bay. Farther back is the railroad lift bridge and, behind that, the Bourne Bridge.

163. When the Army Corps of Engineers enlarged the canal in the 1930s they ran into as many boulders as Belmont's construction gangs did from 1909 to 1914. One of those uncovered was this eight-ton gem of pure quartz. There was a ridge of them lying across the canal's path at Bournedale. This bronze tablet inscribed to August Perry Belmont was placed here by the corps.

164. The Sagamore Bridge photographed from a few feet above the canal.

165. The present Bourne Bridge at dusk.
The railroad bridge is seen in the background.

Bibliography

BOOKS, ARTICLES, AND DOCUMENTS

A Little Visit to the Cape Cod Canal. Buzzards Bay, 1913.

Belmont, August Perry. "Cape Cod Canal and Atlantic Coastal Waterways." Address to the National Rivers and Harbors Congress, Washington, D.C., December 7, 1911. Numerous letters and memos.

Belmont, Eleanor Robson. *The Fabric of Memory.* New York: Farrar, Straus and Cudahy, 1957.

Berman, Bruce D. *Encyclopedia of American Shipwrecks.* Boston: Mariners Press, 1972.

Bourne. Bourne Historical Society Collections.

Brady, Edward M. *Tugs, Towboats and Towing.* Cambridge, Md.: Cornell Maritime Press, 1974.

Brown, Giles T. *Ships That Sail No More.* Lexington: University of Kentucky Press, 1966.

Bunting, W. H. *Portrait of a Port: Boston, 1852–1914.* Cambridge: Harvard University Press, Belknap Press, 1971.

Commonwealth of Massachusetts. Public Document no. 41.

Dalton, John W. *The Life Savers of Cape Cod.* Boston: Barta Press, 1902.

————. *The Cape Cod Canal.* Sandwich, 1911.

"Deepen the Cape Cod Canal." *The North American Review*, April 1916, pp. 501–4.

Drago, Harry Sinclair. *Canal Days in America.* New York: Clarkson N. Potter, 1972.

Dunn, William Warren. *Casco Bay Steamboat Album.* Camden, Maine: Down East, 1969.

Fairburn, William Armstrong. *Merchant Sail.* Center Lovell, Maine: Fairburn Marine Educational Foundation, 1945.

Frizell, Joseph P. "On a Ship Channel Across Cape Cod," *Civil and Mechanical Engineering* (London), July 1871, pp. 41–47.

Goodrich, Carter. *Government Promotion of American Canals and Railroads, 1800–1890.* New York: Columbia University Press, 1960.

————. *Canals and American Economic Development.* New York: Columbia University Press, 1961.

Harris, Robert. *Canals and Their Architecture.* New York: Frederick A. Praeger, 1969.

Harwood, E. C. *Proposed Improvement of the Cape Cod Canal.* New York: American Society of Civil Engineers, Transactions, 1936.

Hilton, George W. *The Night Boat.* Berkeley: Howell-North Books, 1968.

Jane's All the World's Fighting Ships. London: S. Low, Marson and Co., 1950.

Kittredge, Henry C. *Cape Cod, Its People and Their History.* Boston: Houghton Mifflin Co., 1930.

Laurence, Frederick Sturgis. *Coasting Passage.* Concord, Mass.: Charles S. Morgan, 1968.

Leonard, Jonathan Norton. *Atlantic Beaches.* New York: Times-Life Books, 1972.

Lincoln, Joseph C. *Cape Cod Yesterdays.* Boston: Little, Brown and Co., 1937.

Lovell, Russell A. *The Cape Cod Story of Thornton W. Burgess.* Town of Sandwich, 1974.

————. "The Waters of the Cape Cod Canal." Unpublished article, 1974.

McAdam, Roger Williams. *Salts of the Sound.* New York: Stephen Daye Press, 1939.

————. *The Old Fall River Line.* New York: Stephen Daye Press, 1955.

————. *Floating Palaces.* Providence, R.I.: Mowbray Co., 1972.

McCarthy, Joe. *New England.* New York: Time-Life Books, 1967.

Miller, Jacob W. "The History and Economic Value of Canals, with special reference to the Cape Cod Canal." Address to the Society of Naval Architects and Marine Engineers, New York, November 17, 1910.

————. "New England's Interest in the Cape Cod Canal." Address to the New England Society in the City of New York, December 5, 1911.

————. "The Progress of the Cape Cod Canal." Address to the Atlantic Deeper Waterways Assn., Richmond, Va., October 19, 1911.

————. "The Cape Cod Canal." *National Geographic Magazine*, August 1914, pp. 185–90.

————. *Cape Cod and Its Canal.* New York: Boston, Cape Cod and New York Canal Co., 1914.

Morison, Samuel Eliot. *The Battle of the Atlantic.* Boston: Little, Brown and Co., 1947.

New York. Cape Cod Construction Co. and Furst-Clark Construction Co., Contract, December 20, 1912.

Parsons, William Barclay. *The Cape Cod Canal.* New York: American Society of Civil Engineers, Transactions, 1918.

Payne, Robert. *The Canal Builders.* New York: The Macmillan Co., 1959.

Quinn, William P. *Shipwrecks Around Cape Cod.* Farmington, Maine: The Knowlton McLeary Co., 1973.

Reid, William J. "The Cape Cod Canal." Ph.D. dissertation, Boston University, 1958.

Richardson, John M. *Steamboat Lore of the Penobscot.* Rockland, Maine: Courier-Gazette, 1971.

Ryan, Allie. *Penobscot Bay, Mount Desert and Eastport Steamboat Album.* Camden, Maine: Down East, 1972.

Sandwich. Sandwich Historical Society Collections.

Sandwich. Sandwich Public Library Collections.

Sandwich. Sandwich Public Library. Mrs. Harold S. Andrew Papers.

Small, Isaac M. *Shipwrecks on Cape Cod*. Chatham, Mass.: Chatham Press, 1928.

Taylor, William Leonhard. *A Productive Monopoly*. Providence, R.I.: Brown University Press, 1970.

The Cape Cod Canal. Boston, Cape Cod and New York Canal Co., 1925.

"The Cape Cod Canal." *Scientific American*, January 12, 1907, p. 22.

"The Cape Cod Canal." *Scientific American*, September 6, 1913, pp. 184–85.

"The Cape Cod Canal in Service," *Scientific American*, August 8, 1914, p. 94.

Thoreau, Henry David. *Cape Cod*. New York: Thomas Y. Crowell Co., 1961.

Tod, Giles M. S. *The Last Sail Down East*. Barre, Mass.: Barre Publishers, 1965.

United States Army, Corps of Engineers, New England Division, Waltham, Mass., Field Office; Canal Administration Office, Buzzards Bay.

United States Department of Commerce, Bureau of Navigation. 1900–1972. *Merchant Vessels of the United States*. Washington, D.C.

Warner, Arthur. "Please Buy Wall Street's White Elephant." *The Nation*, January 7, 1925, pp. 8–9.

NEWSPAPERS

Boston Globe
Boston Herald
Boston Transcript
Boston Traveler
Bourne Independent
Cape Cod Independent
Cape Cod Standard-Times

Marine Journal
New Bedford Evening Standard
New Bedford Standard-Times
New York Times
Sandwich Observer
Yarmouth Register

Index

Numbers in roman type refer to page numbers. Numbers in *italic type* refer to illustration numbers.